D1453115

I wish that every new essay collection that I read struck me with this kind of honesty, conviction, daring, and intelligence. Kristie Robin Johnson's *High Cotton* adds new experiences and insights to the canon of literary creative nonfiction. Her writing conveys the personal, cultural, and professional with poignant sensitivity. Familial addiction, predatory dating, skin tone, matriarchal lines, reading Audre Lorde, school lockdowns—this is important, fresh work, and you'll want to read it through from cover to cover.
—**Allen Gee, author of** *My Chinese-America*

Both alluringly personal and culturally astute, *High Cotton* examines race, gender, and poverty through the author's experiences as a black daughter, a black mother, and, chiefly, a black woman living in the Deep South. This is a book about finding your place, knowing your place, and the ways you can and cannot escape that place. Kristie Robin Johnson's voice is both lyrical and sharp, soft as cotton, stinging as a snakebite. These essays have charm and power and enviable strength.
—**Aubrey Hirsch, author of** *Why We Never Talk About Sugar*

Among the personal essayist's great challenges—the fundamental challenge— is to somehow be ruthlessly unsentimental about life's traumas and tribulations while still projecting warmth, good humor, empathy, and generosity of spirit: to cast a cold eye on life without being, or seeming to be, cold. In the twenty-one essays (many as piquant as they are brief) that make up *High Cotton*, Kristie Robin Johnson more than meets this goal. But given the vicissitudes that have informed her life and that are her book's principle subject, Johnson's greatest feat is having written the thing at all. That it happens to be so well written is, one might say, the icing on the cake.
—**Peter Selgin, author of** *The Inventors*

High Cotton is a compelling collection of essays that reveal a wide-ranging, pointed curiosity that aims for excavation and revelation. In direct and lively prose, Johnson examines how race, gender, motherhood, sexual violence, poverty, and disability shape her dreams and desires, her realities and responsibilities. Johnson is an uncompromising truth teller, at once vulnerable and fierce, soft and hard. Johnson's essays recount stories of pain forgiven but not forgotten, of love lost but also of love found again and again.
—**Kerry Neville, author of** *Remember to Forget Me*

The pure quality of Kristie Robin Johnson's timely, riveting *High Cotton* often left me breathless. Johnson's dexterous prose makes this vivid collection soar even when taking on the weightiest of themes. I left this book feeling

as if my heart and mind had both expanded. How can life be so hard and so beautiful all at once? I don't know, but I'm sure the answer lies in these pages.
—**Mike McClelland, author of** *Gay Zoo Day*

HIGH COTTON

HIGH COTTON

Essays

KRISTIE ROBIN JOHNSON

Raised Voice Press

Clearwater, Florida

Copyright © 2020 by Kristie Robin Johnson

Published by Raised Voice Press
PO Box 14502
Clearwater, Florida 33766
www.raisedvoicepress.com

All rights reserved. No part of this book may be reproduced without the publisher's written permission, except for brief quotations in reviews.

Front cover photos courtesy of Kristie Robin Johnson
Back cover author photo by Ashley Marks Photography
Cover design by Melissa Williams Design
Interior design by Karen Pickell

This book is a work of nonfiction. Some names of people have been changed to protect their privacy.

Published in the United States of America

ISBN 978-1-949259-09-4 (Paperback)
ISBN 978-1-949259-10-0 (Ebook–Kindle)
ISBN 978-1-949259-11-7 (Ebook–EPUB)

Library of Congress Control Number: 2020931899

Portions of this book were previously published, in different form, in *Bloodletters Literary Magazine, ESME, Lunch Ticket, Rigorous, riverSedge, Split Lip Magazine,* and *Under the Gum Tree.*

for Grady

Contents

HIGH COTTON

Prologue

Our family crest was cotton. You know what I'm sayin'? It's like the only thing we can really leave behind is culture, is music. And dignity and determination. That's what we have.

—Tupac Shakur in an interview with Kurt Loder for MTV,
August 21, 1992

Before I ever took a course in literature, before I was introduced to Langston Hughes or Zora Neale Hurston, before I was captivated by *I Know Why the Caged Bird Sings*, before I ever wrote a single poem or essay, long before I had that first disarming thought that I might actually be a writer, I was stirred by the words of Tupac Shakur.

"Brenda's Got a Baby" debuted in 1991. Tupac's timeless and gritty first single as a solo artist marked the point in my young life when art became personal. At just twelve years old, I was among the masses of young, poor African American girls trying desperately not to become Brenda. As the daughter of an addict, my psyche was seared by Tupac's lyrics in a way that I had never before experienced. Many of his words accost me to this day.

As I have matured, both as a woman and as a writer, my respect for the slain rapper/artist/poet has grown. I intend to write the way Tupac lived—welcoming complication, opening wounds, questioning power, bucking tradition, all without apology. I intend to write from truth so stark it is both hard to look at and difficult to turn away from.

For those of us who don't come from material wealth, survival is our treasure. Our struggles, our heartaches, our insecurities are the canvasses on which we spill our art. Indeed, our crest is cotton, but what we leave behind is gold.

Kristie Robin Johnson

Dope

The first time I ever saw a crack pipe, I must have been five or six years old. My mother was still raw from my father's suffering and eventual death. He had been only forty-four when he passed away, still young and beautiful by human standards. My mother had dubbed him the "black Tom Selleck." He stood six feet, three inches and weighed 220 pounds, and his bare chest boasted a shock of silky, jet-black hair against his copper skin. She joked that near the end of his illness, she'd spent nights at the hospital to guard him from the single nurses. She had been just thirty-four at the time. Seeing my mother winded and widowed too soon, her close friend Liz had offered something to take the edge off, to dull the sting of her loss, to loosen the grip of despair and depression that had begun to suffocate her, to lighten the weight of having to raise her daughter alone. It was cocaine. Eighteen months later, my mother had a full-blown crack addiction. And a crack addiction requires a pipe.

There wasn't just one pipe. There were hundreds of pipes. Literally. Purple ones that seemed to be as tall as me. Short ones no longer than a cigarette. Ancient wooden ones that I imagined were so-called peace pipes of the natives. They were all behind the glass case in what the old folks called a head shop. These were small stores owned by tattooed, bald white guys that catered to vice. Besides crack pipes, the merchandise included TOP rolling papers, a wide variety of lighters decorated with dirty words or bare-chested women, heady sticks of incense, brightly colored incense holders, roach clips, and guns that seemed to be of every size and shape possible. Dazed, as children often are rendered when the curtain concealing adult secrets has been pulled back, I squeezed my mother's hand tighter so that I wouldn't pass out.

By the time I became awed in that head shop, Liz had been dead more than a year.

As time passed, I grew to understand that Liz had been the lucky one in succumbing to her illness (her addiction) swiftly, before it could mangle her youth, beauty, home, job, family, relationships, and reputation into an unrecognizable heap. Liz's exit was brutal but quick. My mother's would be a destructive, dreadful, achingly slow departure. For twenty-two years, she would do battle with this faceless devil. It rumbled gray and heavy like an endless storm tearing roofs from their houses, uprooting trees older than God, sending furniture and cars airborne, leaving lives frayed and unfurled.

I often overheard other grown-ups—grandmas, aunts and uncles, cousins, play cousins, teachers, preachers—refer to my mother as a functioning addict. It meant that, because she could hold down a job in between the first and fifteenth of each month, had not yet lost her home, car, or me, and had not yet sold her body in exchange for crack, she belonged on the highest rung of junkies in the addict hierarchy. It meant that things could've been worse. Much worse.

Because my mother was employed as a substitute teacher for most of my childhood, the mask of normalcy was easy to maintain. She could choose which days she wanted to work and which days she wanted to use. Paydays and the day or two after were always set aside for using. Even though family and friends could readily recognize the pattern, she denied it vehemently. From the time I was five, my mother was a ghost during the first seventy-two hours of any given month. Quick trips to get cigarettes, brief dashes to go cash checks, and short rides to friends' houses almost always swelled into two- or three-day-long crack binges. She always returned silently in the dead of night smelling of musk, stale beer, Newports, and the faint odor of Paloma Picasso perfume, her signature scent when sober.

Another fringe benefit of being a substitute teacher was that her Saturdays and Sundays were always free. Some weekends our house would seem to overflow with partiers—fellow users and dealers along with other enabling friends who smoked marijuana but didn't do blow or smoke crack. While the men's faces seemed to switch like people sifting through a busy revolving door, The Women were static, beautiful constants. LP, TM, CS, and my mother were all in their early to midthirties and stunning. They shined with the kind of beauty and confidence that comes with maturity: knowing exactly what shade of foundation blended best with their tone; wearing clothes that accentuated their curvy legs and hid the stretch marks on their bellies. They had brilliant smiles and large, hearty laughs that echoed self-awareness and self-assuredness. LP was the tallest. She had watery, bright eyes and flawless skin the color of peanut butter. She was a nurse and the single mother of two teenagers. CS was the youngest of The Women, high yellow and heavy chested. She spoke with a near-staccato cadence, her words tumbling over one another. My mother said she was "tie-tongued." TM was thin and waif figured with African features. She had a daughter my age, and we often found ourselves exiled to my room to play while our mothers partied deep into the night. My mother was the shortest of The Women, but the toughest by far. Just a shade lighter than a Hershey's Kiss, she wore raisin-colored lipstick and grew her nails long, painting them a deep hue that resembled red wine. The Women were sophisticated and strong and might have gathered at book club meetings or swank happy hour-affairs had they not befriended cocaine. They would huddle in the den—a room one door down the hall from mine that Mama had repurposed after my father's funeral; it had been my half-brother's room when he lived with us before Daddy died— their heads collectively bowed over a small glass-top coffee table. If you didn't know any better, you'd think they were chemists in a lab, intensely focused on precise measurements and portions. Their tools were typical: razor blades, foil, lighters, a ceramic plate, sometimes a spoon and Pyrex bowl. They made frequent trips from the den to the kitchen and back.

When I got older, I would get a kick out of watching the eyes of men widen to saucers as I told them I knew how to cook crack before my eighth birthday. I became instantly dark and dangerous and intriguing with the candid revelation. Over time, I learned to use it to shock and entice, like a card trick at dinner parties. A small gift, I suppose.

The parties usually crawled from one day into the next, and the adults rarely seemed to notice or mind that they hadn't eaten or showered in nearly twenty-four hours. The Women never looked the same as they had the night before: hair tousled and out of place, mouths dry, skin dulled and ashen, pupils dilated, eyes red with fatigue. Their laughter was reduced to graceless groans, their luster lost to the reverie of inebriation. Regrets slowly filled the slight lines on their faces as they filed out one by one to return to reality, daylight, and the other things they had been desperately trying to escape.

For most of my elementary years this was my version of functional.

In 1991, "Your Mama's on Crack Rock" had to have been the most popular song on the radio, certainly the most popular song blasting from boom boxes and thumping from car stereos on my block. At least it felt like it. For fifth-grade bullies, the punchlines wrote themselves. And I had a bright, blinking target affixed squarely between my eyes.

Despite my mother's struggle, I was an honor roll student, and she feigned sobriety so well that she was appointed secretary of the Parent Teacher Association at my school. I wore my hair in long plaits, was painfully shy, and was often labeled a nerd. Although Mama was able to successfully deceive the teachers and the parents from surrounding neighborhoods, there was no fooling the kids who lived on my block. They knew our secret. Their fathers, uncles, and cousins were often my mother's suppliers and sometimes showed up at our house on weekends. This knowledge was more than enough ammunition for those girls who built their reputations and esteem by tearing down girls like me.

Shenita was one of those soul-eating, fire-breathing girls. Her uncle was a dark-skinned guy known to everyone as Spencer. He was as notorious as a neighborhood dope boy could be. He drove a black Mustang GT and had a gold tooth that could blind you if the sun hit his broad smile just right. He was buoyant and funny and a frequent visitor to the weekend parties. One day Shenita cornered me at lunch. She asked me if my mama was a crackhead. I froze. She said that Spencer was her uncle and that everyone knew my mama was a crackhead. Feeling the curious and bloodthirsty stares of the other kids at the table, I shook my head "no," stared down into the institutional-looking mashed potatoes and mixed vegetables on my lunch tray, and prayed for her to just walk away. When I summoned enough courage to raise my eyes from the food, Shenita was still hovering, now with a spoonful of mashed potatoes fashioned as a catapult pointed directly at my face. "Admit it," she demanded. The "or else" was unspoken but evident in her bulging bug eyes. I felt my own eyes start to fill with tears as a teacher approached us. Shenita put down her spoon, but her eyes lingered on my shame.

By the time I entered my teen years, Mama had lost the house (so much for functional) and we'd moved in with my grandmother shortly after Mama's first stint in rehab. My grandmother's house was situated in the back of a subdivision called Apple Valley. It had been a beautiful slice of suburbia when Granny first purchased her house but was soon bastardized by white flight and Section 8. Dr. Dre's *The Chronic* was my favorite album, and Snoop Dogg's "Gin and Juice" was my favorite song. My mother finally let me get a fashion-forward haircut, boys began to show interest in me, and I was discovering ways to cope with my mother's demons by creating some of my own.

Jesus was my first drug of choice. I discovered Him when I started going to church with my grandmother. She was a freshly converted zealot. She had just been "saved" and wanted to make sure that everyone she encountered from that day forward would be saved as well. Mama and I were first on her spirit-filled hit list. My mother, being both an adult and addict at the time, was hard to turn. But I was easier pickings. Logging in what felt like thousands of hours at Wednesday night Bible studies, Sunday school and Sunday morning services, Sunday evening services, first and third Thursday young adult meetings, choir practices and anniversaries, annual revivals, Vacation Bible School, Mother's Board meetings, Usher Board anniversaries, and a handful of Youth Ministry lock-ins, I was hooked. I became entranced by the prevailing sense of community, held rapt by the notion that all the answers to life's most perplexing queries could be found in the King James version of the Bible. I was completely swept by the choir's sway and melody and the pastor's guttural, ardent invocation. Like most dependencies, I would leave and return and leave and return again, never quite able to achieve that first miraculous high. Sweet Jesus, indeed.

The only thing that seemed as intoxicating as the Holy Ghost was the gaze of men and teenaged boys—full of primitive longing, carnality, desire. For me, men and boys had been peripheral and taboo. They had always lurked around the margins of my life: A dead daddy. A shipped-off half brother. Mama's married, on-again, off-again boyfriend. Drug dealers. Grown men who stared too long at my budding figure. Bumbling, anxiety-ridden, sex-obsessed boys. It wasn't until I became the mother of two sons that I understood the opposite sex to be vulnerable, complex human beings rather than beasts that only existed to be tamed, conquered, or feared.

When I was fifteen, I fell in love with one of those unreachable beasts. His name was Charles, and he was a low-level dope peddler (marijuana by ounces, not pounds; small quantities of cocaine and crack). He was nineteen, lean, muscular, the color of an old penny, and tall enough that my head lay comfortably on his shoulder when we embraced. His eyes were perpetual slits underneath long black lashes, always half-closed. His lips had the shiny brown sheen of someone who smoked blunts all day. His gait was weighed down with disappointment and rage, not unlike most of the other guys in our hood. His mother, like mine, was an addict. He let me wear his gold herringbone chain to make it official. I wasn't a virgin the first time I had sex with Charles, but it was still magical in a way, more emotional than physical. We were two kids escaping the same pain. We were making love. As with most teenage love affairs, the relationship quickly fizzled. I remember returning his chain by way of his younger brother, who was a high school classmate. But I never forgot Charles, his torment, or the sound of his beating heart as we lay naked and pressed together under the cheap plaid sheets on his twin bed while both our mamas were too high to care where we were or what we were doing.

I was supposed to hate boys like Charles, the black-hearted pushers whose main goal in life was to keep my mother hooked and going back for more. But I couldn't. I had seen too much of my own anguish in their eyes. Left despondent and bewildered by underperforming schools, half-assed teachers, overworked or absent parents, an ever-present overzealous police state, and dwindling job opportunities, guys like Charles treated selling dope as just another expected chore, along with dropping out of school and going to jail. This fate seemed an inescapable destiny for kids like us. So, I wasn't surprised to find myself, five years later, giving to birth to a son while his father—a dealer like Charles—paced back and forth in a 6″ × 8″ cage in an Alabama county lockup.

*

Life has a way of becoming less and less black and white as we grow older. The world becomes grayer. Uncrossable lines get crossed. Unthinkable thoughts begin to inhabit the mind. Never becomes maybe, and suddenly we find ourselves changing in frightening, unexpected ways.

After my mother's second failed attempt at rehab, I began to accept the idea that she was always going to be an addict and would always need some kind of vice—somewhere to hide the hurt when life's relentless foot was too heavy upon her neck. I was also beginning to realize that I was my mother's daughter. I, too, was an escape artist, constantly in search of a door marked EXIT. And when neither sex nor salvation was at my fingertips, other substances would have to suffice.

Weed became our Switzerland—a neutral, peaceful stomping ground far less damaging than crack, not nearly as risky as alcohol-fueled hookups with questionable men, and less manipulative than religion. Even though it was illegal, it was tolerable and soothing. Weed mended a great number of the fractures that existed in our relationships. Me and Mama. Mama and Granny.

At the end of the day that my one-year-old son and I moved out of my grandmother's house and into our own apartment, Mama and I celebrated by plopping down on my futon, putting our feet up on the coffee table we'd just assembled, and rolling a joint. I remember her mocking my technique, calling my joints guppies because they were often fat in the middle. I hadn't yet perfected the art. We laughed, and, for a moment, I caught a glimpse of the tough, sassy leader of The Women, radiant again.

While Granny still loved Jesus vigorously, her Holy Roller streak had subsided. Sometimes I think that she may have even viewed Mama's penchant for marijuana as a twisted answer to a fervent prayer. Granny always had a green thumb and loved to watch things grow. So, on a whim, she planted some stray marijuana seeds alongside her squash, zucchini, tomato, and collard plants. Then she loved, watered, and talked to them, and one grew into an ample plant, so big that she eventually had to uproot it for fear police might see the small tree from the street. My mother affectionately called the green, leafy, five-foot-tall bush Bappy.

Marijuana never did what we wanted it to do. It didn't cure Mama. It wasn't strong enough to silence the siren song of cocaine. At best, it gave us brief periods of reprieve and respite from the tumult and chaos of loving an addict, temporary breaks from the arguments, accusations, and tears. It offered us a few days out of each month when neither I nor my grandmother had to worry about whether Mama would return when she asked to borrow the car. It gifted us with a handful of serene nights spent sleeping rather than wondering if she was dead or alive. Granny and I learned to be thankful for the good days and prepared for the bad.

To outsiders, it must have seemed like torture. My grandmother's siblings repeatedly admonished her as an enabler. *Don't lend Pat any money. You know what she gonna do with it.* Most of the time Granny heeded their advice. But Pat was her only child. And there are times when one must believe in their child. How does one just discard their only daughter? The pressure was no lighter on me. On more than one occasion when I was a teen, teachers, counselors, and friends' parents blatantly suggested that I pursue legal emancipation from my mother. But I'd never seriously considered it. My godmother once asserted, *Your mother has never let you finish anything.* But that was only half true. Sure, a violin or two had been pawned for drug money, and gymnastics and cheerleading and piano lessons had taken a back seat to my mother's habit. She disappeared on the night of my first debutante ball and on the day after my son was born. But she was my mother. And I had learned early in life from the demise of her friend Liz that death was certain and quick footed and in inexorable pursuit of my mama. She needed me. And I needed her more than I needed sanity or stability.

The thought that syphons sleep from my nights is that Pat would've been the perfect mother minus the disease of addiction. Sober Pat was the ideal matriarch. Sober Pat sacrificed her light and life and energy watching my father die. She aided home health workers in lifting his over-two-hundred-pound frame to wipe his bottom and change his adult diapers. She risked arrest yelling at the police officer who pulled them over on their muted drive home from the doctor's appointment where they'd learned that Daddy only had six months to a year to live. Sober Pat allowed my six-year-old hands to part her texturized hair into small square sections with a giant, neon-blue Goody comb so that I could practice plaiting and French braiding when my Barbie dolls no longer sufficed. Sober Pat and I often took naps together on the couch in the den; she lay on her belly, face pressed into the cushion, and my small frame snuggled on her back, soothed by the warmth emanating from her slumbering body. We performed this ritual until I was about eight years old and too big to sleep on my mama's back. Sober Pat baked cupcakes and brought them to my classroom on my birthday. And when I was in middle school, she let me have a sleepover with three of my friends and spent forty dollars on a tub of Superman ice cream from a fancy ice cream parlor in the mall. When Sober Pat had money, she spared no expense. We vacationed at Disney World and Myrtle Beach. Sober Pat purchased every edition of *The World Book Encyclopedia* from 1980 until 1990, and whenever I asked her a question that was academic in nature, she fired back without raising an eyebrow, *Look it up*. In doing this, she taught me to love learning and to take charge of my own education. And often, when Pat wasn't sober, it was those volumes in which I took refuge until Sober Pat returned. Indeed, it was Sober Pat who envisioned me as a writer decades before I could see myself as an essayist and poet. It was she who encouraged me—her shy, self-doubting eighth grader—to submit a poem for publication in the Sego Middle School anthology; when a sixth grader chose my piece to perform in the school talent show, I was flabbergasted, but Sober Pat wasn't surprised at all. It was Sober Pat who believed the doctor when my son was diagnosed with autism and helped me shuttle him back and forth to daily speech and occupational therapy appointments and held my hand during those first Individualized Education Program (IEP) meetings while I wept.

As selfless as she was, Sober Pat tried to nurse her own fading dreams as well. She'd always confessed a lifelong desire to be a prison warden and, at fifty-three years old, Sober Pat became a Peace Officer Standards and Training Council (POST) certified corrections officer with Georgia's Department of Juvenile Justice.

She was almost perfect.

On June 6, 2006—twenty days before her fifty-sixth birthday—Mama went to sleep and never woke up, claimed by a massive stroke according the Columbia County coroner. TM was the only one of The Women who called to offer her condolences.

*

And even as a crack fiend, Mama / You always was a black queen, Mama.

That's the line that always breaks me. It picks me up and then drops me from a hundred-story skyscraper. Tupac's "Dear Mama" plays on a loop as I scoot my patio chair closer to the sun. I want to feel the heat on my toes. I wash down an ill-gotten Adderall with a lukewarm Corona. It's my second drink today. I balance my laptop on my thighs and stare into a blank Word document. These are my Mother's Days now—motherless and teeming with memories too vivid to relive, dreams too distant to imagine. I wish that Mama were still here. I wish that Granny could've held her daughter one last time confident in her complete sobriety. I wish that Mama had started using in 2004 instead of 1984. Then, perhaps, a better-educated society would have looked at her and seen a person with an illness in need of help and not a lost cause from which to flee. I wish that Mama had been born white and preferred painkillers; then she would've been at the center of the Republicans' heartfelt plea to address America's opioid epidemic rather than the target of disproportionate and oppressive sentencing laws. I wish Mama were sitting in the chair next to me, round faced and glowing and laughing, holding an impeccably rolled joint between her thumb and index finger, legs crossed at the ankles, shoeless toes swinging just a hair above the concrete ground. I wish she'd bring the joint to her puckered ebony lips, inhale, and blow small white clouds above her head in the shapes of halos. I wish.

Skinned

By my mama's own admission, I was bleached. Not dipped in Clorox at birth, nor chemically lightened as, for instance, Michael Jackson allegedly was. Nope. I was bleached the old-fashioned way—by having a baby with a person a few (or several) shades lighter in the hopes that your child will emerge more fair skinned than you.

I know my mama loved my daddy. But she talked about his beauty in a way that flirted with worship, fizzed with envy. It was as if his physical attractiveness surpassed all. Having been only four years old when he passed away, I remember an outlandishly tall, copper-colored man with a hearty bass in his voice and hands as big as my torso. She remembered a god—broad shoulders, tapered waist, toned legs covered in a mist of fine midnight-colored hair, teeth so perfect that she initially believed them to be dentures—and though he was noticeably African American, his skin was far lighter than her dark chocolate tone. Mama said that she longed to have his child from the moment they met.

Mama pitied her own skin—its darkness, the way it only got darker in the sun, the way it resembled that of Aunt Jemima more than Lena Horne or Dorothy Dandridge. She believed many racial falsehoods in her lifetime, but one of the most destructive was the notion that "white is right." Since slavery, it's been common knowledge in black communities that fair skin could afford one access to white amenities not made readily available to the darker masses. Mulatto slaves often served their bondage in the shade of the big house while browner beasts labored in the fields. The lightest African Americans could pass for white and many times used that gift to clear a path to freedom. So-called high-yellow gals enjoyed/suffered the adulation of both black and white men, their hue being so dangerously close to the European standard of beauty. Over time, softer pigmentation came to equivocate success—higher salaries, more desirable zip codes, esteemed educations; you may not have been white, but you were nobody's tar baby. And though these myths held little truth, girls who were born in 1950 and were darker than a brown paper bag often suffered the silent shame of feeling less than, not pretty, not enough.

My mama had been one of those less fortunate girls—she was too far from white. The color of her skin fermented a silent shame within her, along with an irrational disdain for light-skinned black people. One of her closest friends during her formative years in the late fifties and early sixties had been her next-door neighbor, a girl so fair that her eyes appeared sometimes hazel, sometimes a greenish hue, and her hair was a dark brown that got lighter in the summer sun. They'd spent time playing paper dolls and hopscotch during the schoolyear. But from June through August, Mama's friendly attitude soured. Mama alleged that her neighbor's mother never let her come out to play during the high heat of summer afternoons for fear of her precious yellow girl baking into a brown anomaly. She was only allowed to go outside in the evening as the sun was going down. That she deliberately ducked daylight to avoid looking African made Mama fume. Mama said that she spied her summertime "frenemy" peeking from behind the curtains watching all the "darkies" shape red clay into mud pies and scatter for a game of hide-and-seek. She admitted she picked a fight with her foe as soon as the girl's mother let her come outside. Mama beat her up because she couldn't *be* her.

By the time Mama met Daddy, she'd settled into her blackness. Thanks to public figures like James Brown, who cut off his conk in favor of an Afro and penned the anthemic "Say It Loud: I'm Black and I'm Proud," and the impact of the Black Power movement and the Black Is Beautiful campaign, Mama embraced her racial heritage but still resented the lasting effects of colorism. She begrudged them so much that she refused to allow her offspring to be subject to the taint of skin as dark as her own. She hoped that Daddy's slight mulatto features paired with her more coffee-colored tone would produce a smooth, raw pecan color for her baby. Her hunch proved to be true in the tenth month of 1979 when I was born.

Like many African American infants, at birth my skin was very light. It would be a few months before my permanent hue would settle across my small form. Sensing her insecurities about my color, my great-grandmother teased my mama, chiding, *Yeah, she gonna be a little black gal*, as she examined the curl of my ears and the skin covering my tiny cuticles. Mama often recounted with pride and laughter the day that she went to the grocery store with me (still only a few weeks old) and my great-grandmother and bumped into an old family friend. As is customary, especially in the Deep South, the old friend openly admired me, the new addition to the family, gushing, "Oh, she's so pretty! Is her daddy Puerto Rican?" Mama felt two feelings: (1) flattered at the compliment, because she believed that her baby was, indeed, lovely, and (2) pissed at the insinuation that she had nothing to do with that beauty and at the further suggestion that no black man could have possibly been capable of mating with her and creating a kid this fair. In her trademark curtness, Mama replied, "No. He's a Puerto nigger!" The old friend, frozen in disbelief, turned to my great-grandmother seeking confirmation. She looked at the friend and dryly stated, "That's the baby she brought home from the hospital."

Color colored my childhood. And while I never felt the haunting regrets that Mama held about her skin, I did spend hours imagining what it would be like to be light skinned, maybe even white—to crawl out from the constraints of my toasted caramel coating and be the object of everyone's affection; to always see myself on TV and on *Vogue* covers and on Paris runways; to date the quarterback; to never dread mirrors; to be regarded as the prototype. Despite having the benefit of Daddy's complexion, I still clamped clothespins on my nostrils, praying the pressure might reduce the thickness of my wide nigger nose. I kicked the monstrous habit of tongue sucking by replaying my granny's admonition that the act would leave my lips fat and ugly. Every time I scraped my knee or scratched a bug bite, Mama massaged a mixture of cocoa butter and bleaching cream into the area to prevent a hideous cockroach-colored scar from ruining my tan tone. When I became a teenager, it was brutally apparent that light-skinned girls with light eyes and long hair would always be black boys' first choice; if a black girl happened to be half-white, half-Hispanic, or half-Asian, she had hit the genetic jackpot in terms of beauty and popularity. Halle Berry and Mariah Carey were, for me, who Lena Horne and Dorothy Dandridge had been for Mama—stinging reminders of our humble station as darker black women:

mammies, maids, background singers, less attractive besties, earth mothers, pretty-for-a-black-girl outsiders, hardnosed bullies, unassuming girls next door.

A bit luckier than Mama and her contemporaries, I did have a golden-brown American goddess to worship. I had Whitney Houston. I remember watching—no, studying—the "I Wanna Dance with Somebody" video in awe and amazement. Whitney's magnetic smile and bouncing, blonde weave hypnotized me. Her skin, the same shiny pecan as mine, glowed with the unfettered joy of those white girls who typically appeared on the cover of *Seventeen* magazine. I loved her. I didn't have to want to be her because I *was* her. My eight-year-old psyche soared with confidence. Finally, a star who resembled the rest of us. There would be others—Mary J. Blige, Janet Jackson, Queen Latifah—but none who so wholly altered my perception of my own reflection, who repaired my fractured black swan wings.

I grew to accept my natural tan, my plump lips, and my nose that seems to spread farther with each smile, even while in the shadow of America's unending preference for faces brighter than mine with less melanin and anger, less sun-kissed anxiety, less untraditional grace, less threatening joy, less undeserved pain. I didn't inherit Mama's color-based loathing. I freely befriended high-yellow boys, redbone girls, biracial kids, all God's children. At times, I coveted their unearned pedestal, but hate never took hold of my heart. I often laughed at Mama's scowl when women with fair skin and Caucasian features won beauty pageants and snickered at her jeers when she accused high-yellow African Americans of behaving as though they were superior to other black people. By the time I reached adulthood, Mama's paradoxical relationship with her skin color had become a routine wonder. No soul waved the flag of black pride higher than Mama, yet she hadn't been able to stomach the thought of bearing a child as black as her. She offered little more than measured spite to bright-faced black women, yet her soul mate had been a black man far lighter than her.

When I became pregnant with my second child, Mama announced that she was *gonna take that baby out in the sun to get some color!* My husband was several shades lighter than me and came from a bloodline of very light-skinned Northerners, some so fair they had gray eyes and dark blonde hair. This unsettled Mama. The same way that there had been such a thing for her as too dark, one could also be too light. I realized then that Mama sought some mythical perfect color—a tone noticeably African, but not charred enough to stir memories of blackface and minstrel shows and gently swinging nooses and not white enough to let you forget your oppression. Mama died before she could take my baby out in the blazing Georgia sun, but I never let him forget.

I have only one regret. I often wish that Mama would have lived long enough to witness Michelle Obama's graceful reign as *our* First Lady—an undeniably black woman, nearly as dark as she was. I wish Mama had been there to sip mimosas and toast to the new black First Family on Inauguration Day with me and my light-skinned in-laws. She might have shed some of the shame and hate that marked her upbringing. She might have seen a bit of herself in Michelle's chocolate face, elegant stature, quiet power.

I often wonder what role color will play in the lives of my two sons—a honeyed-peanut-butter-colored seventeen-year-old and an eleven-year-old the same shade as a cup of café au lait. Demographers and researchers predict that in just a little more than twenty years' time, current racial minorities will make up a clear majority of the US population. Some have even suggested that the cures to racism and colorism are just a few generations away because the entire populace will bear a neutral beige hue as a result of increased miscegenation. The idea of a color-blind, race-neutral America is tempting and even intoxicating if you allow yourself to get lost in the dream. But it is just a dream, not a reality that I can foresee in my lifetime or that of my children. I can, however, foresee a future where my boys don't have to look far to see themselves represented in the popular culture. Today, black men across the color spectrum—from dark-skinned thespian Idris Elba to biracial professional athlete turned activist Colin Kaepernick—enjoy a great deal of visibility in the mainstream spotlight. The challenge for my children's generation will be to garner enough social capital and personal agency to ensure that there are more positive reflections than harmful stereotypes of their image made available to the masses. The distinction between shades of black will not matter to them the way it mattered to me and my mother; but the contrast between white and nonwhite will paint their lives in broad and sometimes startling strokes.

Now as a woman well into my thirties, I treasure my skin as a blessing, never a curse. I used to roll my eyes with frustration every time I heard a rapper sing the praises of a half-black/half-Asian girl. I fought to hide my discomfort whenever I heard a black man say he preferred an exotic woman or foreign chick. These declarations of desire for faces unmarred by overt blackness used to incense me. How dare one regard my straight-from-the-boat features as ordinary, unbeautiful? Learning to love my color was a happy side effect of learning to love myself. True beauty is about acceptance, and acceptance begins at home. Mama struggled with self-love, but even as she fretted over color, she always made it clear that her love for me was unconditional. I get darker in our hazy, humid summers, and I lose some bronze during those few mild weeks before spring that we laughingly call winter. I remain lovely through it all, not because I'm lighter than Mama or almost the same color as Daddy, but because my brown is a testament to survival and resolve.

Broke, Not Broken

You slide your phone out of the back pocket of your jeans, check the time, and realize you've been standing in line for seventeen minutes. The old you would have complained by now, demanded to speak to a manager. But the new you is humbled by the lady in front of you who has been waiting just as long while managing a young toddler and a baby. You've passed some of the time playing an impromptu game of peekaboo with the baby, who is resting happily in a well-worn carrier. You openly admire the cloud of chestnut curls on his head and take some fleeting joy in his laughter and innocence, something you haven't allowed yourself to do in a while. The carrier's scuffs, scratches, and dingy fabric lead you to deduce that it is secondhand at best. The toddler, who's spent most of the time taxying between her mother's arms and the floor next to the baby in the carrier, is wearing a bright orange shirt that looks to be about one size too small.

When you first walked in, you took stock of the building, the waiting room, and its inhabitants. Right away, you noticed that the building was old and outdated. Many of the ceiling tiles were a yellowish-brown color from apparent water damage. There were no windows, no sunlight spilling into the drab space. The waiting room wall was lined with open cubicles, each with a plastic blue chair in front of it and a telephone. Some even had telephone books next to the phones, which reminded you that this place, this situation, these people were all relics compared to the mainstream world that existed outside these pitiful walls covered with posters touting the benefits of breastfeeding, warning of the consequences of food-stamp fraud, and dutifully listing the phone numbers of agencies that help with utility bills. Each sign was printed in Spanish as well as English. An out-of-order Coke machine stood to your left and two check-in windows loomed directly in front of you. You immediately noticed that the windows were bulletproof, as though those in charge were all too aware of the infuriating level of frustration that just one visit to the Columbia County Division of Family and Children Services (DFCS) could cause. Somehow, you'd forgotten.

A little over a year ago, your divorce was finalized. It had been one of those instances in life that began with great trepidation but ended with great relief. You had learned to take care of yourself and your two growing boys, to pay the mortgage, car note, and light, water, cable, and phone bills on an annual income of just under $40,000 along with $500 a month in child-support payments.

Then five months ago, you got an email that changed everything. It was an acceptance letter from Georgia College. They thought you were a decent writer; in fact, so decent that they offered you a slot in the upcoming class of creative nonfiction writers. Since you were sixteen, writing had been your recovery, therapy, sanity, and sanctuary. Writing anchored you through a reluctant career change from politics to higher education, seven years of a bad marriage, the numerous struggles of raising a child with disabilities, the sudden death of your mother. The possibility of writing professionally was too dangerously close for you to pass up. So, you secured a graduate assistantship to cover tuition and scheduled a meeting with the chair of the Master of Fine Arts in Creative Writing program.

Two months ago, your stomach churned to the point of mild nausea while you waited for the president. Well, not *the* president, but Mr. E was close enough. He was your boss at the community college where you worked. The envelope in your hand containing your official letter of resignation might as well have weighed five hundred pounds by the time Mr. E welcomed you into his office. You couldn't contain your nerves as you explained to him that you'd been given a rare opportunity that girls who were raised by addicts and became mothers too soon don't often get. You felt your shaky cadence quicken as you told him about your passion for writing, the anticipated eighty-mile each way daily commute, the graduate assistantship, the impossibility of juggling full-time employment. You were both exhilarated and scared shitless.

Three weeks ago, you crunched the numbers, and realized that, even with student loans, child support, and part-time employment, you still needed help. Help—an idea hidden within the fabled concept of American ingenuity, buried underneath the Horatio Alger myth and the fictitious self-made man. Because you had been brought up in a society and culture built upon these tales, help was just another dirty four-letter word to you. To have to say it out loud, even to yourself, almost made you physically ill. You thought you'd outgrown this part of your life. Help was for direction-less, uneducated saps. Help was for the girl you used to be—the college dropout, the unmarried pregnant teenager. Up until this moment, you had not realized that you judged your younger self so harshly, perhaps unfairly. You'd spent the last fifteen years patting yourself on the back for returning to school, completing bachelor's and master's degrees, finding a good man and getting married, landing a decent job, not once but twice. Too often, you had failed to acknowledge all the help you received along the way. Your mother and grandmother helped care for your child for free, allowing you to complete your education. An eager and generous profes-sor encouraged your career path, even recommended you for jobs. A col-league and friend thought of you first when a coveted opportunity in your field became available. You had been given a tremendous amount of help. It didn't always come from Uncle Sam, but it always came. Remembering this, you got over your self-righteous vision of the woman you thought you were, you pulled up the Georgia Department of Human Services website, and you completed the application for food-stamp benefits.

Which brought you here to this line, these sad walls, the impene-trable glass that separates you from the help that you need. When you finally reach the front of the line, you recognize a familiar warmth on the face of the lady behind the glass. She reminds you of your grandaunt—bifocals and a kind smile. Even though there are two windows, she is the only one at the desk. And, also like your great aunt, she does not move with any speed. In your hands, you are holding copies of your sons' birth certificates and your separation letter from the college. As you approach, you direct your words toward the holes in the glass, "I'm returning my verification documents," mindfully using the departmental jargon in the hope that you might be treated a tad better than the average applicant. The kind-faced lady barely gives you a second look. She asks for your Social Security number. You give it to her. Then she types several key-strokes on her keyboard. The computer has a blinder on it that keeps you from seeing what's on the screen, and you think to yourself that this office, this whole damn system, is designed to keep people in their place—behind the glass, blind to the process, beneath the threadbare line between poverty and barely getting by. Then she gets up and drags her body over to the copier behind her desk. You notice how her body rocks from left to right like a boat as she makes the tiny voyage. She seems exhausted, and it's only a few minutes past eleven in the morning. She returns to the window with your original documents. You ask her what the next steps are. She curtly replies, "You'll get a notice in the mail in a few days."

You walk out the office and head to your car thinking August in Georgia is never kind. It's always been stifling, unbearable, humbling. The distance from DFCS to your house is a series of winding state roads lined with towering pine trees, several modest homes built on lots measured in acres, a rock quarry, the county fairgrounds, two Walmarts, and no fewer than twenty subdivisions boasting four- and five-bedroom homes on intolerably small lots meant to lure ex-urbanites into their planned neighborhoods promising less crime, excellent schools, the goddamned American Dream. This trip reminds you of the reason you moved to Columbia County. Outwardly, you did it to ensure your children an alleged better education. Inwardly, though, you wanted to escape the uneven, jagged face of poverty—schools situated in the hearts of housing projects; boyfriends with precarious futures and pockets full of dime bags; hand-me-down clothes from the daughter of the bank president your grandma keeps house for; Christmases replete with drugstore toys and knockoff jeans and sneakers; monthly visits to the greasy payday loan spot; mamas with too many jobs and never enough money; mamas' mamas who never get to taste the sweet liberated air of retirement, who work right up until the day they die; hopes that hinge upon lucky numbers, neon-colored scratch-off cards, and birthing a world-class athlete or singer or rapper. You came because you wanted out. You wanted to never look back.

When you get home, you realize you are not the same person who left this morning. You are a taker now. Or at least, that's what you're convinced the world will think when you head out grocery shopping next month with your telltale Electronic Benefits Transfer (EBT) card.

The few days promised by the lady behind the glass turn out to be eleven. The envelope is heavy, like the credit card offers that flooded your mailbox when you were employed full time. You open it slowly, not really wanting what is inside, but knowing that you need it. The last time you felt this way, you were nine and you were opening a birthday gift from your grandma; you knew it was the winter coat that you needed, but you were secretly wishing for a Nintendo Power Pad to peek from underneath the tissue paper and bows. The EBT card itself is rather pleasant to the eye. It features an artist's rendering of two ripe peaches still attached to the tree, surrounded by bright green leaves. The words GEORGIA EBT are sprawled across the front in white and yellow capital letters, a bold reminder that this is not a luxury. The words remind you that you are now dependent upon the state. They remind you that there is a cost to pursuing dreams, and sometimes the price is your pride.

You put off using the card until there is nothing in the pantry but a six-month-old box of cereal and two jars of peanut butter (which remain unopened mainly because you and your oldest son have peanut allergies). You have two months' worth of benefits on your card, which amounts to $658. When you were an underemployed, undergraduate, twenty-year-old single mom, that money was a godsend. Today, it's an inconvenient mirror casting an unwelcome reflection. You plan this trip to the supermarket meticulously. You will not wear makeup. You will put on jeans, sneakers, and an old blue sweatshirt with two small bleach stains on the right sleeve. You make a list that only includes food items—fresh fruits, vegetables, meats, canned foods, dry goods—things that can be paid for with food-stamp benefits. You will not be purchasing other nonfood staples such as paper towels, toilet paper, trash bags, or soap. Over the past two weeks, you've created a somewhat narcissistic narrative in your mind that the clerk and the people waiting in line behind you will judge you less harshly if you don't seem too put together or appear to have resources other than that which the government dispenses. You want to look sufficiently poor.

You consider going to a store outside of your neighborhood, but you decide against it. The EBT card is less conspicuous than the actual paper food stamps of your youth. You can only recall seeing them on a few occasions on trips to the grocery store with your grandma, and you are pretty sure they weren't hers. You're pretty sure she purchased them from a neighbor or cousin who needed cash more than they needed food, probably near the end of the month or around the holidays. You remember the old stamps looking like pages in a coupon book. It was almost impossible to use them without other shoppers noticing. The EBT card is not much different from anyone else's debit or credit card. The average person can't distinguish one from the other and probably doesn't care. But you are convinced that every blue, brown, green, and gray iris in the vicinity will be fixated on your personal financial crisis.

The first few minutes in the grocery store are normal. You examine the bananas, looking for a bunch with a slight streak of green running the length of each peel. You select the milk with latest expiration date. You get the boys' favorite brand of cereal and the marinara sauce that makes your spaghetti sing. Then you get to the meat department. This is where you'd normally start to cringe at the prices and start thinking about how many gallons of gas you need to put in your car this week and the data plan on your phone. But calm settles over you as you pick up a package of split chicken breasts, the chill from the plastic wrap numbing the tips of your fingers. It dawns on you that you can get the chicken and the ground turkey and the pork chops and the swai fillet. It's the first time in a while you've been able to shop without that small voice in your head reminding you of all your other expenses.

You feel euphoric until you make your way to the register. Never once in your life have you agonized so over which checkout lane to go through. You cannot use the express lane; you have way more than twelve items. A quick survey of the other aisles reveals four choices: the nerdy girl with the thick-rimmed glasses who's always smiling, the older lady with shoulder-length gray hair who always attempts to strike up a conversation about the items in your shopping cart, the short middle-aged woman whom you've always pegged to be a manager, or the beautiful Hispanic man with the bad tattoo on his forearm. You choose the bad-tattoo guy. His lane is closest to the door, and he isn't a stranger to regrettable decisions. You take labored but invisible breaths as you place your items on the conveyer belt. After the last pack of ramen noodles makes its way to the scanner, you pull out your wallet and hold it so close to your chest that you're sure the customer behind you thinks you fear getting mugged right there in the middle of the Food Lion. You delicately slide your EBT card out of the wallet face down, so that only the reader strip is visible. As you swipe the card, you notice that you've forgotten one detail—your nails. Your painted, manicured nails. They're Boston College red, to be exact. Only you and bad tattoo guy know your secret, but that small voice in your head that used to warn you about your bank account balance is now telling you all the things bad-tattoo guy is thinking: *She got money to get her nails done, but she can't buy groceries. A damn shame. I feel sorry for her kids. I bet she got at least four.*

You make it out of the store, but tears start to well up in your eyes. Pushing the cart across the parking lot, you want to scream into the rich, chiseled faces of Paul Ryan and Mitt Romney and Ronald Reagan and any other person who shares their backward perceptions of poverty. This is no fucking victory lap! There is no triumph in surviving and not thriving. There are no "queens" here. There are, however, more than forty million Americans, most of whom work, who share this experience with you. As you drive home, you're fighting back tears as you remember that you're lucky to live in a nation that offers help, as despicable as it may sound to some, your old self included. There is only nobility—not shame—in not allowing children to go hungry. The fact that we can and often do help others in need should be a national point of pride, not some humiliating burden. You know that this is not your forever, but it is your right now. You roll down the windows and let the wind catch your pain as you watch the store disappear in the rearview mirror.

Kristie Robin Johnson

Men Forever

"Baby, black women have been *men* forever." The words tumbled from my mouth with the confidence and sass of a woman twice my size. One of the perks of being a counselor-in-name-only at a technical college was that you could dish out just about any quip in response to a student's concern and pass it off as wisdom. I offered up this particular gem about the legendary stoicism of African American women to shore up the strength of a young female student. She was a twenty-year-old white girl. She had giant brown eyes and wore thin-rimmed glasses that made her eyes look even bigger. She was pretty when she smiled but had bad teeth, so she had mastered the art of the toothless grin. Her auburn hair was cut into a shoulder-length bob. There was an understated quality to her presence; my grandma would've called her homely. You could tell that she hadn't been told she was beautiful enough by her folks, if she'd been told at all.

The student came into the counseling center that day still reeling from the night before. Her live-in boyfriend/baby's father had gone, in her words, ballistic. He hadn't hit her, but they'd had an argument so bad that she'd put him out of their mobile home. She said he banged on the door so relentlessly that she had to call the cops. She began to tremble when she said this hadn't been the first time he'd become belligerent. He'd been out of work and drinking heavily. He was spiraling, and she'd become desperate. She was in school full time trying to become a paramedic. She worked part time at a day care, making just a dollar more than the minimum wage. She'd been waitlisted by the state for food stamps and childcare assistance for her own one-year-old son. Stuck in a single wide with an angry, jobless man, a helpless infant, and no sign of better days on the horizon, this girl wanted help. And more than that, she needed hope.

27

There wasn't much actual help I could offer her, and I'm not sure that she found my response hopeful. But I did give her honesty. Her story hadn't been much different from the stories of women I'd known all my life or from my own story. At twenty-two, a daily combination of NoDoz and coffee had been the only savior that got me through an 8:00 a.m. humanities course after working the overnight shift at a call center. It had been trying, but it was the most moral and legal way to provide for me and my disabled two-year-old. My mother had once taken a job in construction for a year to subsidize my father's wages, which were being garnished for back child-support payments. Rather than panic after her husband woke up one morning and decided he wasn't ready for the responsibility of a family, my grandmother had enrolled in night classes to get her GED and taught herself shorthand to increase her employability. My great-grandmother had found the resolve to spend decades of her life scrubbing floors and ironing clothes for rich white families during the day, then going home in the afternoons to take care of her own five children and, later, five of her grandchildren, all while enduring a marriage to a man who cheated and drank as hard as he'd worked. I could empathize with the young lady, but I wouldn't coddle her. I told her that instead of wrapping herself up in the unfairness of her circumstances, she'd have to man up, make some sacrifices and hard decisions. I was blunt. I told her that her son's father was an adult and had to fend for himself. She needed to focus on herself and her son's safety. She said that she still had a decent relationship with her parents, so I encouraged her to reach out to them despite what judgments they might've made. I gave her some tips to help expedite her applications for state benefits and sent her on her way.

After she left, I boiled with resentment. What gave her the right to complain when things got a little tough? What made her think that she could live a life without expecting tribulation? I never could. The thoughts gave rise to a startling callousness. I felt guilty for having thought them, but they came from my core. I realized that I'd been cold to her because very few people had ever shown warmth when I'd experienced the same struggles—being a single parent, stressed-out college student, and one of the countless working poor all at once. I couldn't give what I'd never received.

What was more, I belonged to a class of women who'd been historically viewed as more ten-point buck than timid doe. It had never been unusual for black women to work extra shifts, raise children that weren't theirs, wake up before the sun and lie down after midnight, head households by themselves, hold down second and third jobs, mow lawns, change tires, pay bills. However, it had been rare to see black women cry, exhibit vulnerability, or seek professional help. Breaking down had been a luxury afforded primarily to our white counterparts. We learned to make light of it, dismiss it as weakness. Now when I contemplate my life and the lives of the women who brought me forth, I've come to question the true cost of our fabled tenacity. Are we better for having hid our emotions, swallowing years of unsaid words, uncried tears, and unexpressed pains?

Vinie

I first heard the name Vinie Johnson at a family reunion in 2007. My mom had been dead a little more than a year when my two grandaunts and I climbed into my white Buick Rendezvous for the forty-five-mile trek from Augusta to Lincolnton. It was the first time that we'd all been in a car together since the subdued limo ride to my mother's funeral. Even though it's only about an hour-long drive, we had traveled at least fifty years into the past by the time we pulled up at the small community center. Perched atop a slight incline off the winding state road, the building looked more like a cabin desperately resisting modernity. Genuine hardwood floors, exposed pine beams in the ceiling, brick walls, and a stone fireplace lent a rustic spirit to the festivities. Early September is still summer in Georgia, and we'd grown accustomed to the humid heat that caused us to sweat in the shade—dampness soaking the backs of our knees and the undersides of our breasts. We were thankful for the structure's air conditioning in spite of its antiquated charm.

Family had become a strained concept to me. Having lost both my grandmother and mother in a four-year span, I'd been plagued by a sense of disconnection, as if I had no roots, no real home to return to if I ever ventured off. In hindsight, that's probably the only reason I agreed to go to the reunion—to discover a bond, reestablish roots.

On the eastern wall of the complex, someone had painstakingly attached a roughly nine-foot-long roll of white paper with our extended family tree printed in black ink. I got so close to the paper searching for names that my nose almost touched the parchment. I found Zula Martin Robinson (1906–1997), then ran my fingers along the thin lines branching out from her name and landed on Christine Robinson Kennedy (1925–2002), and from there rushed down to Patricia Kennedy Johnson (1950–2006), and settled finally upon Kristie Johnson Gregory (1979–living)—four generations of mothers, none breathing except me. Then my fingers retraced the line, back above Zula, above Zula's mother, to the very top, to a name I'd never seen: Vinie Johnson.

After a half hour of wall scanning, mingling, and hugging distant relatives, the crowd of about sixty was corralled by my cousin who'd organized the gathering. Dressed in traditional African garb, she welcomed us and proceeded to tell us the story of my oldest known ancestor. Vinie had been a slave, held captive right there in Lincolnton. The only known record of her existence had been a brief newspaper clip that described her attempted escape after one of her children had been sold to a nearby planter. My cousin told us Vinie had slipped off in the cool night and swam the length of a lake trying to retrieve her child.

Mesmerized by the account, I conjured up a version of Vinie in my imagination. She was a glistening brown—the same color as fine cognac—bronzed by the noonday sun beating down on her humped back as she picked cotton. A crown of thick, black coils sprouted from her scalp. Long, dark piano-playing fingers stretched from callus-covered palms and arms dotted with healed scars from briar scratches and mosquito bites. She had lips and a nose like mine. Her eyes were shaped like plump almonds and they sparkled like crystals, far brighter than her dreary existence. Her calves were smooth and strong as any man's calves. And Vinie's heart pumped fire, wished for freedom with every beat. I imagined that the wails of her baby being dragged away consumed her, filled her with a courage unexpected. At nightfall she had set out, her daughter's cries still ringing in her ears, rattling in her chest. She took to the chilled waters desperate to find and soothe her girl, the birthright of every mother. And for the crime of thinking herself human, the lash split open her back. Twenty times.

I took my vision of that woman, my third great-grandmother, and made her my guardian angel. Knowing that her blood flowed through my unworthy veins ignited a new purpose within me. I was never the same.

Zula

Born in 1906, Zula was Vinie's granddaughter and by all accounts just as brave and hard-edged as her grandmother.

My earliest memories of my great-grandmother were of a short, caramel-colored woman whose skin was already wrinkled when I was born. She had a variety of gray wigs that she stored on Styrofoam heads on a shelf in her bedroom, and her house was always impeccably clean. On Christmas and birthdays, she'd give me a crisp twenty-dollar bill and tell me not to spend it all in one place. Every time I visited her, it was my job to prepare her spit cup. She chewed tobacco, and I had to stuff a paper towel into a bright red Solo cup that she used to spit tobacco juice and remnants into. Everyone called her Mama Zula and, for me, she was a living monument.

Just like all black women of her time in the Deep South, she bore the burden of segregation and state-sanctioned racism. Zula was a young mother during the height of the Great Migration and, while the lure of northern opportunities (better pay and fewer lynchings) was too attractive for many to pass up, my great-grandmother wouldn't budge. Even after her husband had secured a job in Philadelphia, she stood her ground. Some friends and family called her foolish, even cruel, for not relocating her family. I believe she was valiant—to not flee, to not cower in the beet-red face of hate. No number of flaming crosses, WHITE ONLY signs, or discriminatory poll tests would be enough for her to uproot her family from the home they'd worked for that was rightfully theirs. Aided by her eldest son's military service and subsequent access to a Veterans Affairs (VA) home loan, she and her husband, Richard Sr., had secured the small lot on Boy Scout Road in Augusta and built their humble, three-bedroom home from the ground up. Zula remained fixed for her children and demonstrated fearlessness.

Only one person ever confessed to seeing my great-grandmother cry. According to my mother, when Richard Jr. died, Mama Zula sat slumped on the side of her bed and in a hushed, solemn voice she whispered into the air, "Well, when you gave him to me you didn't tell me how long I could keep him." Then she sighed a hefty, son-mourning sigh and shed silent tears before preparing herself to bury her firstborn son.

The Rest of Us

Zula gave birth to three daughters: Christine, Lillie, and Mary. The three of them produced seven children in all, five boys and two girls. Christine's only child, Patricia, was my mother. Zula's hands helped mold all of us into the sturdy creatures we became. Christine was the first single female homeowner in the family, and my mother was the first (male or female) to earn a college degree. Lillie and Mary had long and productive careers in manufacturing and health care. And it seems that each of us has been built with cinder blocks, not clay.

Fragility is perilous if you're born poor and black. Fragility won't wake you at 4:00 a.m. to make the five-mile walk to a minimum-wage job to feed your kids. Fragility won't weather the storm of throwing all your earthly belongings into a black plastic garbage bag in the dead of night when you decide that your face can no longer serve as a punching bag for the man you love. Fragility won't lend you the resolve necessary to keep you from crumbling when you get the call telling you that your son was gunned down by a rival gang member. Fragility won't provide enough energy to take you from your first eight-hour shift to your second job when your feet ache and body begs you for rest. Fragility won't protect you from your own feeble mind when the thought of suicide loiters two seconds too long.

Zula and the millions of other black women like her had been fortune-tellers. They knew what we'd be up against. So, in many ways, they bred us like boys—roughed us up, forbade tears, prepared us more for work than marriage, valued smarts above beauty. When I was fourteen, my best friend and I got caught sneaking gin from my mother's liquor cabinet to spike our Kool-Aid. We were kids. We thought it was funny. When our exaggerated giddiness and sneaky behavior revealed our teenage delinquency, my mother didn't lecture us, ground me, or call my best friend's mom. Instead she called us into the kitchen, placed the fifth of Seagram's Gin on the kitchen table (the bottle a little more than half-full), told us to take a seat, slid two glass tumblers in front of us with the expertise of a seasoned bartender, and poured full glasses, making us drink the gin straight until the bottle was empty. The next day, she reveled in our headaches, nausea, and vomiting.

When I got in my first fight in middle school, I came home scuffed up, clothes torn, hair in complete disarray. I begged my mother and grandmother to let me stay home from school the next day—to heal some bruises, on my body and on my ego. There had been rumblings among other kids that my opponent's friends intended to jump me the next day. I told Mama and Granny everything. They didn't care. No daughter of theirs was going to run or hide. The next morning, I was attacked at the bus stop by five girls. I arose from the melee beaten, but not punked.

We were reared to live life bending without breaking. And from our foremothers' sacrifices, the following generations emerged as a grand amalgamation of mixed blessings. African American women are earning graduate degrees at a breakneck pace; yet mothers still make up the majority of people living in poverty. We are entering the halls of Congress and of state assemblies in record numbers; yet we are still disproportionately underrepresented in all levels of government. We fervently search for that elusive work-family balance as the divorce rate steadily rises. In fact, black women remain one of the most unmarried groups of Americans. We aimed for the pristine perfection of Clair Huxtable and have landed somewhere near the supreme complication of Olivia Pope.

I often wonder who I might've become if I hadn't been raised to shun open emotions, to favor independence before love. I might've been a more understanding wife with a more forgiving heart. I might've been less competitive and combative. I might still be married. I might've been a kinder mother. I might raise less hell and hug my sons more often. I might not rail about disheveled bedrooms or greet straight A report cards with indifference, telling my kids that I don't reward people for doing things they are supposed to do. I might've been a more empathetic person. I might've considered the heart of the woman lying in bed alone before deciding to sleep with her husband. I might not need a cocktail or a blunt or an edible or some other mind-altering chemical to go to sleep at night. Yet I have no regrets about the way I was brought up. Vinie and Zula and Christine and Patricia made me a fighter and a survivor; but I understand now that our strength doesn't lie in our masculine silences, our constant pretending to be invincible. As long as I breathe, my foremothers will be with me and, together, we will learn to evolve, to emote without shame, to love without reins, to swiftly forgive, to offer others the mercy we didn't receive, and to someday shed this thick skin that made us men from the outset.

Humanity at the Grovetown Nail Spa

After seventy-three days and 140 miles of mind-numbing asphalt lined by pines and oaks and cedars, after so much ink and paper and so many computer screens telling me whether I am rich or poor or worthy of Uncle Sam's largesse, after more than two months of waiting to be told whether my kids can eat or have their teeth cleaned or get vaccines and answering stupid questions such as *What are you going to do now?* and *What about the kids?* when they really want to ask *Who's giving you handouts?* and *How much debt have you racked up?* and wanting to look them in the eye and say, "I'm a fucking writer and you're a fucking coward," but not saying this, instead nodding and smiling without showing my teeth and saying, "We get by just fine," after eleven Tuesday mornings spent in a run-down school cafeteria plagued with rotting ceilings and mold (my anxieties at panic levels) sitting and conversing with undereducated holy women almost as old as the decrepit building suffocating me and then holding hands in a circle and praying with them in their Old Testament ritual to their Old Testament God, all just to pay my tuition, and eleven Tuesday nights black as sin, exhaustion weighing me down, my sheer will keeping the Sonata in between the yellow lines, after ten weeks of taking the leap and stepping out on faith and proving a short, yellow, biggity ex-husband wrong, I find myself at the storefront, its neon blazing OPEN, not caring about cost as though I am rich, head bowed just slightly because I know that I am not, walking in—at first gaze seeing a row of dutiful hunched backs tending to ankles and heels and toes—smelling the weird aroma of acetone mixed with hot wax mixed with fried chicken from next door that is somehow relaxing, and I can't help but smile (all teeth) at the meaty, pink, thick-skinned women who remind me of the salmon we talked about during my last visit several months ago, when I met Rosie, as pretty and naive as her name, who held me captive with stories about being a native Alaskan Eskimo, and how her mother moved all the way to Georgia to make tired, insecure women feel attractive, and how her daughter's father needed to grow up, and how she had a crush on one of the construction workers across the parking lot, while she firmly pressed her thick digits into the flesh of my bare calves, kneading the weary dough, and then I remembered how her skin touching mine lulled me into a trance and away from autistic teenager meltdowns, sexless divorced life, fruitless work, and how, while she blew warm air from her mouth through her tightened lips over my thin-skinned and freshly painted toes, I confessed, "I am a writer," and she believed me, and, in that moment, she was Magdalene with silk onyx hair engaged in holy sacrament, and I was unworthy, but then, waking me with a jolt, a voice calls out, "How we help you?" and I reply, "Mani-pedi—Is Rosie working today?" and her big-boned mother yells, "Roseee!" and from the back she appears, directs me to a chair, runs water into the shiny white basin, delicately lowers my left foot then my right into the bubbling brew, and, once they are submerged, a thousand hours of ache escape the balls of my spent feet, and Rosie looks up at me, grinning wide and glowing from our thick unforgiving summer, jet-black wisps of her hair glued to her temples, and I think I see something akin to love.

The Truth about Old Men and Worms

There was no innocence more dangerous than the innocence of age.
    —Gabriel García Márquez, *Love in the Time of Cholera*

Old men will give you worms. It was a myth often uttered as sheer fact throughout my childhood and well into my teen and adult years. The first folks I can remember saying it were my grandmother and her contemporaries. They were not saying it directly to me. I would overhear the quip at raucous barbecues and all-night card parties where moonshine and Schlitz Malt Liquor flowed freely. One lady would say to a younger lady, "Girl, you still messin' wit Ray from Royal Street?"

The younger girl, mostly out of respect plus a little fear and a bit of embarrassment, would reply tepidly, "Yes ma'am."

Then one of the older ladies would shoot back with a raised eyebrow, hand on hip, "Chile, you know old men will give you worms!"

The entire flock would roar with drunken glee. This scene would repeat itself many times throughout my life with different settings and different characters, but the same dooming sentiment about the consequences of dating older men remained.

I grew to dismiss the tall tale of my upbringing as unscientific silliness and just one of those crazy things that old people say. Then at twenty-three, I met a man. A forty-eight-year-old, short, light-skinned car salesman. His yellow face, interrupted by a thin mustache and goatee, wore an enthusiastic smile. He approached me and my mother as we eyed a slate-gray Saturn Ion.

"You looking to buy today?" he asked, getting right to the point.

"Yeah, I've got a trade," I replied, pointing to the 1996 gold Saturn I inherited from my grandmother when she died.

He introduced himself as Ken and took us on a test-drive of the Ion. When I determined that the payments on the Ion would be too expensive, he suggested an earlier-model silver Saturn SL.

Ken came off as arrogant but generous, shrewd but kind; and being not nearly as dastardly as the average car seller, he gave me a good deal on a dependable vehicle. While I was signing the last of the paperwork to finalize the purchase, he asked me to dinner. I told him we could have lunch.

This had been my free-meal dating phase. Any potential suitor who asked me out got an instant "Yes" regardless of height, weight, race, color, creed, nationality, religion, or age. I wasn't turning down any free meals. If the date turned out to be awful, I didn't go out with the individual again. The way I saw it, I got a free meal out of the deal, and the guy got an opportunity to present his best version of himself. I'd tried other tactics—only dating guys my own age, only dating men who tucked their shirt into their pants, not dating at all and waiting for God to send my Boaz (that didn't last long)—and I'd grown weary and lonely. Being a young single mother, I feared my options were much slimmer than the average girl my age. The free-meal method had been my ridiculous way of improving my odds of finding a partner. Ken was attractive and affable and, at the time, I had no idea that he was twenty-five years older than me.

Even though he came off a tad presumptuous, candidly suggesting that I'd soon meet his kids, and didn't have many nice things to say at lunch about his former spouse, Ken was still charming enough to earn a second date. The second date turned into a third, and before I knew it, I was seeing somebody. Sometime between the third and fourth dates, Ken revealed his age. He already knew that I was twenty-three, because he'd processed all the paperwork during the vehicle purchase. I knew that he was older, but I thought he was in his late thirties, maybe forty. I never imagined that he was almost fifty years old. It didn't seem fair to stop dating a person just because he turned out be older than I had expected. The fact that he was forty-eight hadn't changed anything. He was still a stable homeowner with a decent job and defined biceps who was nice to my kid and my mom. We continued to see each other.

About a month passed and, as it goes with relationships, expectations blossomed. I began grappling with the idea that Ken would want to have sex, sooner rather than later. That's when the voices started. Every time Ken touched me, I could hear my grandmother and her friends giggling in my head, *Girl, he's gonna give you worms!* I knew it didn't make any sense, but it rattled me. I felt like a complete lunatic. I searched for psychological explanations. Maybe his age was a deal breaker for me, and the haunting old wives' tale stuck in my head was a manifestation of that fact. Maybe the incantation was rooted in some form of self-sabotage. Perhaps deep down, I feared being in a healthy relationship, so the auditory delusions served as a pathway back to my familiar single misery. Ken feigned patience, but I knew better. Middle age unravels men—makes them question themselves, their stamina, their prowess, their purpose. Graying hairs, widening bald spots, and aching joints tell them that they're old. Their impulse is to fight time, to strive against the inevitable by proving themselves still valuable. Sex with a twenty-three-year-old, for Ken, was a reclamation of an allure he felt slipping away. Sex with a forty-eight-year-old, for me, was a venture into forbidden territory confirmed by the fables of my youth.

I needed proof to settle the cacophony between my ears. My grandmother had already passed away by then, so I wouldn't get the satisfaction of hearing her admit that there was no truth whatsoever to the tomfoolery. I needed the confirmation of a woman who had lay down with an older man and had risen worm free. Luckily, my own father had been ten years older than my mother, and she was still around, and I had a friend who was dating a guy who was almost eleven years older than her. Neither of their situations matched the twenty-five-year age gap that I was contemplating, but at that point I just needed someone to say that they knew, without any doubt, that old men would not give you worms.

Both my mom and friend suggested that I might be insane for even asking, but they also both admitted that they had been chided with the same superstitious warnings. My mother's eyes lit with an uncommon tenderness as she recounted her courtship with my father. Between long, sumptuous drags of her menthol Newport, she reminisced about the sweet parts first—gifts of expensive perfume and flowers, lovers' conversations full of longing and secrets, the best sex of her life. Then she cut her eyes at me sharply, turning off the faucet of good feelings. "Kristie, older men can be jealous. And possessive." The warning erupted from a memory she didn't detail, but I could tell that it had been a dark place nonetheless.

My friend, who had been seeing her older beau for more than a year, found her experience refreshing. She beamed as she boasted about his maturity and work ethic. She was also a single mom and had shared my panic, imagining that her child would render her less desirable, less marriable. She said that her boyfriend's extra years made him patient; plus, he had children of his own, which gave them a common experience, solidified their bond. These stories helped to ease my mind. Ken started to feel more like a genuine possibility. Eventually, I gave in.

In your early twenties, love is just another high—no different than marijuana or ecstasy or coke. You drown in the flood of your own emotions, float away on the rush of skipped heartbeats and bare skin and promises made after midnight. And you relish every second of it. You want more. You return to the source repeatedly. *Make it like the first time* is your only pitiful request. Later in life, you realize that love is a wild beast to be tamed—impetuous and brazen. You find that love must be regimented, controlled. You spend days trying and failing to tie her to a sycamore with a worn, fraying rope. You waste countless nights in futility attempting to muzzle her miserable howls. You wrestle with her till blood is drawn, knuckles bruised, eyes fattened by her wretched claws. You no longer recognize yourself. You learn that she will not be tamed, so you build a fortress to keep her at bay, hide behind the safety of its walls. I was getting high while Ken was taking cover in the castle.

We were happy at first. Ken wasn't a romantic or affectionate man, but he was reliable. He was confident and duty driven, and I admired that. My youthfulness excited him. I decided that this must be true love. After nearly a year and a half of dating, Ken surprised me with a diamond ring on Christmas Eve. He'd hidden it in the corner of a large shoe box and placed a twenty-ounce bottle of Pepsi in the box to weigh it down so that when I picked up the package, I'd think it was the leather boots I'd asked for in November. When my frantic, curious hands finally arrived at the small, square, mustard-colored box engraved with Jeweler's Bench in gold letters, I opened it and squealed. I didn't wait for a question. I decided that this was his proposal and soon we'd be married.

Dr. Saunders's office was dark and moody, like a lounge or an opium den. The only light in the room came from a single window letting in the gloom of a rainy day and a small lamp situated on an end table next to the leather couch where Ken and I were seated. This was the first of the four premarital counseling sessions that we had to complete to save fifty dollars on our marriage license. Even though this would be his third marriage, Ken despised the idea of counseling, but he didn't mind saving the money. He'd chalked it up to four half-hour meetings where me and a white woman would discuss *my* issues, while he'd sit back and listen to us squawk.

As was the case with most people meeting us for the first time, Dr. Saunders was taken aback by our age difference. After harping on the statistical odds of our marriage, or any marriage, actually lasting, which were dismal, she zeroed in on the age gap. She leaned in, looked at Ken with a strident determination and asked him if he understood that I wouldn't always be a young twenty-something. She asked him if he was prepared to watch me grow old. Reverse psychology. I fully understood that that question had been for me, to trigger a vision of a wrinkling Ken. I dealt with the notion of watching my husband grow older by not thinking about it at all. I'd spent the entirety of our eighteen-month engagement obsessing over reception venues and bridesmaids' gowns and menu selections and guest lists. I'd busied myself by scheduling fittings and choosing stationery and perfecting every detail of the ceremony. I'd deliberately overwhelmed myself with the wedding to detach from the impending marriage. I was afraid. But facing the fear of marriage meant facing an even greater fear—that I might be alone forever.

Then, in March, just weeks before our May 12 wedding date, a home pregnancy test read positive. For the first time, Ken felt old instead of older. He'd be fifty-two when the baby was born and seventy by the time he or she would graduate from high school. The gravity of that test stick had leveled me. As Dr. Saunders continued to pepper Ken with questions about my vanishing youth, I rested my arms on my tummy, our baby not

41

even the size of a bird resting inside, and stared out the window watching raindrops bounce off the asphalt while I imagined browsing coffin colors with a college student.

The vision in Dr. Saunders office turned out to be an omen. Less than a month after our wedding, my mother died. I chose a cream-and-rose-colored coffin for her. I wondered if I'd broken her heart by marrying Ken. She'd never been against it, but she'd always been concerned. She had constantly reminded me that we had no common interests, no mutual friends, no shared goals, no real reason for coupling other than loneliness, convenience, and now, this baby. Love alone wouldn't carry us.

I read somewhere that tragedies often bring couples closer. A collective suffering can rock the foundation of the strongest relationship, causing the pair to cling to each other, depend on one another's strength like never before. I kept waiting for my dead mother to drive us into each other's arms, to make Ken ask me about my dreams or read something I'd written, to make him say "I love you" for no reason at all, to make him look at me and see more than sex three times a week and mediocre cooking, to make him want to pray with me at night and cross his thin legs in meditation with me in the mornings, to make him find my tears a sign of sincerity and not weakness. I kept waiting.

We named our son after my mother: Patrick for Patricia. He emerged in early November a nicely filled-out little creature with plump cheeks and bright black-brown eyes. I'd been so sad while I'd carried him—mourning my mother, waiting for my husband to replace the love that evaporated with her last breath—I'd prayed daily that he'd enter the world joyful, not the inheritor of my despair. What was more, I needed this boy to make us a family. Something out of a Norman Rockwell painting, where the mother prepared a pot roast and made biscuits from scratch all while wearing fire-engine-red lipstick and a string of pearls, and the father rolled up his sleeves and doted on the children, everyone sporting wide toothy grins. I needed him to make real the artificial mirth I'd been passing off as bliss to outsiders.

Patrick wasn't magic. He brought the typical delight that babies bring: the comfort of nuzzling tiny hands and feet, the sedative bond of nursing, the wonder of watching a living being grow. But he didn't make me and Ken kinder to one another. He didn't stop the recession from devouring his father's savings, ambition, and masculine pride. He didn't transform me into the docile domestic goddess that his father would've preferred. He made us true partners in parenting, but he didn't make us friends.

Ken and I spent 80 percent of our time and energy on the boys. Day care drop-off, parent/teacher conferences, birthday parties, doctor and dentist appointments, Christmas shopping, karate lessons, and back-to-school supply lists consumed our lives and dominated much of our conversations. Another 18 percent of our time was spent either agonizing or arguing over bills. By the third year of our marriage, we had three kinds of debt: bills that were past due, bills that were way past due, and bills that we didn't even consider paying. The 2 percent of time that remained for one another was marked by silence and obligatory lovemaking.

Ken girded himself with obstinacy—showing up to customer-less car lots every day, month after month, hoping for a merciful cloud to break. I avoided our problems by staying occupied. I finished a master's degree, took a second job teaching, joined community boards and advisory panels to fend off the reality of our waning intimacy, the staleness of struggle, the twenty-five-year chasm that painted me as an oblivious dreamer in the eyes of my husband and rendered him a rigid old fogy to me. Every four or five months, I'd suggest counseling and he'd decline. His reliability, steadfastness, and structural integrity that I'd appreciated so much in the beginning started to look more like stagnation—the inertia of passing years and decades, the inability to change even in the most harrowing of circumstances—when utilities got cut off, when the rent was late, when I went days without speaking to my spouse because I was depressed—even as time changed me.

By Patrick's fifth birthday, the economy had brightened. We were able to pay down some of our debt, and Ken and I transitioned from being unhappy renters to unhappy homeowners. The new house did add a spark to our daily tedium. Ken had less time to criticize my parenting skills or weight gain with a new lawn to manicure. I had less time to roll my eyes at his sage advice that always began with *You know this ain't my first rodeo* while picking out new furniture.

Our home was in a new development. The subdivision was only halfway completed when we moved in. We noticed an elderly man in a bright red pickup truck going door-to-door. He was trying to sell water purification systems. Perhaps out of some unwritten code of solidarity amongst men who make their livings on commissions, Ken made an appointment with the gentleman to pitch his product to us. He certainly didn't opt to give him an audience because we were potential buyers. We were doing better, but we didn't have that kind money.

The salesman pulled up in our driveway a little after seven in the evening. It must have been autumn because the sun was already going down. Ken answered the door and the man trudged in, managing a slight limp, holding what looked like a magician's briefcase in one hand and pulling a wheeled black crate with the other. I don't recall his name, but I never forgot his face. He had to have been at least seventy years old, and the crooked lines in his peach-tinted flesh spoke a lifetime of uncertainties. His glassy gray eyes whispered a melancholy for days past. His hair was a glistening white, wavy but thinning. He grimaced as he sat down at our kitchen table, and his feeble fingers trembled as he demonstrated the water softening properties of his product. He was a man in decline, tired and still working. He was polite and did his best to appear jubilant, even when we told him that we couldn't purchase the system. As he gathered his brochures and bottles and test tubes, packed them up, and made his slow, rickety walk from the kitchen to the front door, Ken didn't offer to help him. He knew that the salesman's dignity and ability to stand upright on his own were two of his last prized possessions, and he let him hold on to them that evening.

That night a disturbing premonition took hold of me. I envisioned Ken at seventy-plus years, feet worn from fifty-five-hour workweeks beating pavement and cajoling would-be car buyers, exhaustion hanging under his eyes, tired but still working like the water system salesman. I didn't fear watching him grow old as much as I feared watching him grow angrier, colder, more despondent, more distant from the world, more resentful of his path. I didn't want to watch him die a death weighed down with regrets.

I never cheated on Ken and I don't believe that he ever cheated on me. That must count for something.

Two years after we moved into the new house, Ken finally agreed to counseling. We went to a different white lady this time. My insurance covered eight sessions. The first six appointments followed the same self-defeating pattern. We showed up in separate cars (most of the time we were coming from our jobs), tried to curb the awkwardness of the wait in the lobby with small talk about *True Blood* and *American Idol*, then plopped on the therapist's couch—Ken disgruntled and me depressed. We began to talk, I started to cry, Ken was indifferent, the therapist assigned exercises for home, we never did them, I scheduled the next appointment.

The seventh appointment was on Valentine's Day. Clouds hung low to the earth, threatening a rare Southern snowfall. It was cold, but not a bitter chill. Ken and I were fatigued, mentally and physically: weary of the fruitless therapy visits, the redundant battles over bills and the boys, the mammoth-sized tension in the air between us. We were spent and no longer trying. Ken didn't even bother to remove his jacket when we sat down. Again, we began to talk. I remember the conversation feeling bloodless, like we were two empty cadavers void of our former humanity. In a last exasperated gasp, I looked at Ken's stone face: "Why couldn't you just try? For me?"

Then the counselor interjected, "Ken, what Kristie is really asking is, do you love her?"

In retrospect, she probably only asked the question because she thought she could predict the answer. She thought he'd say, "Of course," even if it was only a half-truth. But, he didn't. He was silent. His face went from concrete to the softness of an apology, as if to say, *I'm sorry, but I don't love you anymore.* His silence was eternal. The truth seemed to shock even him. He'd searched his heart for something that turned out not to be there. When I got home, for the first time in seven years, I pushed my diamond engagement ring—the one that had changed my twenty-four-year-old world forever—past my knuckle and into my palm. The wedding band followed.

Ken didn't come to the eighth and final session. I sat on the couch alone, eyes red and puffy, mourning a marriage that had been cursed from the start.

All my life, I've wondered why someone would make up such foolishness: old men giving women worms. It's as repulsive as it is unbelievable. And while Ken certainly didn't leave me with any intestinal tapeworms attached to my gut, feeding off me, he did leave an intractable emptiness that ate moon-sized portions of my esteem and courage and faith for years to come. During our ten years together, Ken had rarely said that he loved me. He routinely put down my cooking and insisted that I "learn how to be a wife." Valentine's Days, birthdays, and even a Christmas or two went by giftless. There was no kissing or hand holding or deep conversation.

I had always felt that something was wrong with me, that I wasn't doing enough to make him happy. Then it dawned on me. My grandmother had recycled this parable from her own childhood to protect me and my mother and the other younger women in her life. She came from a time when women weren't guaranteed equal standing or even safety, for that matter. Happiness in a marriage was a long shot. In a world where women had many fewer social and economic options than we do today, concocting stories about certain types of men had been more of a defense mechanism designed to keep women from becoming shells of themselves stuck in loveless, unfulfilling situations than a random, funny punchline. Saying *old men will give you worms* was the same as saying, Baby, be careful—some men will take advantage of you; some men will take your money; some men will hit you and then beg you for forgiveness; some men will put you down to feel better about themselves; some men will tell you that they love you when they love someone else; some men will leave at the first sign of trouble; some men will break your heart. While Ken wasn't the worst husband, he certainly was not meant to be *my* husband.

Today, I can appreciate the concern of my elders, no matter how it's expressed. And maybe one day I, too, will place an indignant hand on my hip and cock my head slightly to the right and admonish somebody's daughter, "Girl, you know that old men will give you worms."

On Her Back

Consider the amount of time a woman will spend on her back during her lifetime. Looking up, searching the sky for the eyes of God. Eyes shut tight, trying to imagine the next moment or trying to reimagine the last. Eyes wide open, counting optimistic clouds or staring down doom. Resting, fighting, working, wondering, all while parallel to the horizon.

My mother said I came into this world kicking and screaming, limbs stretched in every direction, searching for oxygen, sustenance, sun. She lay on her back as they announced, "It's a girl!" According to her account she smiled a satisfied smile, examined her offspring—running her fingers through a cloud of jet-black curls, counting ten perfectly formed fingers and toes, kissing my plump rose-tinted cheeks—and then nodded back off into a medically induced twilight.

She always said that she wanted a daughter. Even before the pregnancy test came back positive. Even before she met my father. Even knowing the sometimes high price of girlhood and womanhood for herself—the permanent vulnerability of our bodies, the mountain of double standards thrust upon us, the labels we endure when we choose to live free—still she wished for a girl.

Though none of us can truly recall it, I imagine my first days were spent on my back or nestled up against my mother's warm breast, my father's soothing heartbeat, my brother's tense, bony arms, or my grandmother's antique shoulder. A lucky little girl, being passed from arm to arm, learning the world through downward-facing smiles and giant, joyful laughs. Some girls aren't so lucky.

47

II

His name was Marty and, at eighteen, he was the oldest boy who'd ever liked me. I was fourteen and just plain stupid, as fourteen-year-olds tend to be. It's quite possibly the worst kind of stupidity, rooted in an unshakeable confidence, fueled with a child's energy, housed in an adult's body, and encouraged by other teenaged idiots.

How I met him escapes my memory, but I know that it wasn't beautiful or fairy-tale-like. Though stupid, I was smart enough to know that Prince Charming wasn't showing up in a wifebeater, basketball shorts, and last year's Air Jordans.

Two weeks shy of my fifteenth birthday, he talked me into letting him come over while my mother was still at work. Completely aware of the expectation of sex, I opened the door. His expectation reflected everyone's expectation. Girls who were popular, or who wanted to be popular, as was the case with me, didn't stay virgins forever. Unrealistic prudes waited, fearful girls whose lives lacked risk or grit. A lot of girls felt pressured to have sex the first time by their boyfriend or partner. Much less interested in Marty's desires than what other girls on the block might think, I readied myself for the high school fame (or infamy) bound to come. Not only was he older, but he was a fair-skinned black boy, reminiscent of El DeBarge, with wavy, not nappy, hair. Legitimate crush material for a teen girl in 1994. In the eyes of those popular girls, I'd be rebellious, experienced, and therefore, envied.

I let him kiss me on my mother's sofa. The taste of his tongue repulsed me. Like a cigarette. I let him put his hands between my legs and underneath my bra. When he was "ready," he shot to his feet and gestured towards the hall, and I led him to my mother's bedroom. The white daybed adorned with hand-painted pink and purple flowers across the hall in my room seemed too immature for an experienced eighteen-year-old. The nerves didn't appear until I was lying on my mother's bed. I thought he'd lie down next to me, but he didn't. He remained upright and pulled my hips to the edge of the bed, both of us naked only from the waist down.

I held my breath and closed my eyes and then abruptly opened them. I really wanted to see his penis. A more clinical desire, not lustful in any way. The only penises I'd ever seen up until that moment were the underwhelming portrayals found in Renaissance-era sculptures and paintings and the well-hung men that appeared in my best friend's dad's porn collection. Marty's penis wasn't one or the other. It was fatter and shorter than I expected, more spherical than cylindrical. Like a small can of condensed milk. I silently concluded that dicks are a lot like the guys attached to them. They come in a variety of colors, shapes, and sizes. The thought made me feel weird and slutty, like I shouldn't be thinking it at all. Like I'd suddenly slipped into the mind of a woman my mother's age. I started to have second thoughts but rejected the impulse to tell him to leave. Stupid.

He squeezed himself into me and thrusted forcefully for about nine or ten minutes. I felt absent for the whole ordeal. Flat on my back, I looked right through him, his yellow face a transparent void. I focused on a crack in my mother's bedroom ceiling. It hurt. But not too much. I wondered how I might reinvent this moment. My first time. What lie could I tell to make it more romantic? More chivalrous? Finally, he stopped heaving and wore a certain intensity on his face. I don't know how I looked. But I felt indifferent and just glad that the whole thing was over, as if a necessary evil had been completed at long last. As he pulled his shorts back onto his waist, I had the feeling that I wouldn't see Marty again. And I wasn't upset by the thought at all.

About a week later, walking to the corner store with two friends, a girl and a guy, we started to discuss our weekend plans. We decided that since the girl's mom had to work the night shift on Friday, we'd party at her house. The only question remaining: how to get the booze. Far from being good kids, we didn't consider ourselves delinquents either. We were the middling class of teens. We drank, smoked, cut class on occasion, and stole CDs from the Sam Goody in the mall. But we didn't gangbang or sell drugs or carjack people like some of our peers. After bouncing around a few ideas, the boy perked up with deviant glee.

"We could just get Marty to buy it."

"Does he have a fake ID? He's only eighteen," I said confident and quick.

"He doesn't need a fake ID. He's twenty-four. He buys beer for me and my cousin all the time," the boy replied.

My almost fifteen-year-old heart stopped. The word "twenty-four" bounced around in my head. I felt like I was trapped in an echo chamber. "Twenty-four, twenty-four, twenty-four . . ." I needed to be tough in that moment. I pretended to be unfazed on the outside. On the inside, my soul emptied all of its contents right there on the asphalt. Everything that made me soft or innocent or young had been poured out of me with my friend's revelation. Suddenly, the act that had made me bold and grown-up decimated me. I learned what it meant to feel violated. I felt dirty and dumb and desperate to return to being the girl I had been before.

III

Darkness and unconsciousness are the same. Completely black. Absolute and silent. Drifting in and out of the world, my eyelids felt like they weighed fifty pounds each. And the rest of me was heavier. I couldn't even shift my own weight when the nurses came in every few hours to administer shots in my hips or check my IV fluids or vital signs. When I mustered up the strength to open my eyes, I saw the soft fluorescent light above my hospital bed. The last thing I could recall was struggling to swallow some abysmal liquid charcoal concoction underneath the bright, invasive emergency room lights. I thought I heard a white man telling my mother, "She's not out of the woods yet."

Paralyzed under the weight of my reality, the only thing I could accomplish with my conscious mind was to stare up and think back to the day before, the night before, the whole year before I found myself useless and plundered my grandmother's medicine cabinet.

I'd managed to flatten myself with about eighty iron supplements, a bottle of Tylenol, and a half bottle of quinine. Hence the horrible tar-like substance I was forced to drink. Hence the slipping in and out of consciousness, the four-day-long hospital stay and consequent quack visits, and the looks of disbelief that would slowly spread across people's faces when I told them why I'd been in the hospital.

The question always was, and still is, *Why?* And the only answer I have ever been able to conceive is that, at sixteen years old, I had run out of reasons to live.

I lay there in the darkened room listening to the intermittent beeps of monitors, counting the steady drips of clear liquid into my IV bag. The previous day came back in flashes with glowing centers that faded swiftly into a blurred fog. Abbreviated vignettes appeared in between long, laborious blinks. Slipping into a formfitting dress, easy to remove. Packing a nightie in my backpack. Pretending to walk to the bus stop. Hopping in the car with two older guys. The hot breeze rushing against my eyelashes on the drive to a cheap motel. Letting the last swig of strawberry-flavored Boone's Farm roll down my throat before the blinds blotted out the sun. My mother's voice engorged with rage, rejection, shame. The longest, hottest shower, praying to melt and slide down the drain with the day's filth. The medicine cabinet mirror, the answers on the other side.

My grandmother's Pentecostal faith taught me to view sex as sinful, to hate myself, my fragile humanity, my flesh. God was supposed to be an experience that bubbled up in you and saved you from your own primal urges. I always thought God or Satan or something was supposed to appear when your soul started to part ways with your body. But my only caller was Silence. Guess it wasn't time.

Complete consciousness returned along with irrepressible tremors, ice-cold skin, and rampant nausea. My best friend in the world stayed by my bedside as long as her mother would let her, pulling my hair away from my face with one hand, holding a mauve-colored kidney bean–shaped plastic basin in the other, as the poison poured out of me with violent force. And when I was finally empty, and still alive, I spent the last night in the hospital dry heaving over the toilet.

IV

Pregnant isn't something you get. It's something you become.

When I became pregnant, it was the final atrocious act in a line of colossal fuckups: Moving out of my godmother's house because I wanted more freedom after she took me in as a college freshman as a favor to my mother. Getting evicted from my first apartment after freedom didn't quite work out the way my rowdy-ass roommates and I had planned. Racking up thousands of dollars in traffic tickets and credit card debt. Flunking out of Georgia State University. And now, arriving home, no degree in hand, penniless and pregnant.

The only good thing, according to everyone except me, was that I still had options. By options, they meant option, and by option, they meant abortion. It was quite simple. I should just get up, go to the clinic, and take care of the problem. (I should also mention that no one ever had the balls to actually use the word "abortion.") And then I was supposed to pretend nothing had ever happened.

Choosing to stay pregnant became the first truly great defiant act of my life. Later I'd view motherhood as kind and selfless as well. But it began as pure rebellion, the epitome of audacity—a nineteen-year-old baby thinking that she could take care of a baby of her own.

As the seasons slowly changed from a perverse August heat into a long Georgia autumn, then into the chilly frost of early spring mornings, my wayward belly grew and grew. Rounder in the face of nosy church mothers. More plump to fuel the tall tales of gossipy coworkers. Ballooning without shame to the chagrin of fellow former debutantes. Heavier on the thwarted hearts of my mother and grandmother. Me and the baby inside me, outlaws.

A boy. He came on the fourth day of March. Deliberately slow, I think. After eighteen hours of fruitless labor, I found myself on my back in the operating room: Familiar bright lights. Strapped to the operating table, half-drunk from Demerol for pain and another drug to reduce blood pressure. My mother in scrubs, jubilant, not bitter. *You're gonna feel some pressure. Okay.* Wailing, more defiant than pitiful. *Just like your mama.* Lying there, I wondered, Could it really be this simple? Just a little bit of strain and discomfort, and bam! Welcome to Motherhood? Unreal.

Soon after the delivery, the nurse brought my boy to me. All cleaned up, he was a ray of light swaddled in flimsy linens with a pink-and-blue-striped cap perched atop his head. I'd never found faith in a thing so small; his entire hand wrapped around my thumb. Up until that moment, I don't think I'd ever found faith at all. With him in my arms, I looked up and closed my eyes, in search of a promise. Inhale. *Please help me do this.* Exhale.

V

I followed the directions with a surgeon's precision. *Stay on J. Dewey Gray Circle until you see the large glass building on the left, the Women's Diagnostic Center. They're on the first floor, second suite on the right.*

I pulled into the parking lot, and a wall of a thousand sunlit mirrors stared back at me. I wondered aloud why one would put a bearer of grim news in a building like this? Perhaps a woman needs to look herself in the eye before her entire world becomes unrecognizable.

I walked into the small rectangular waiting room, signed in, and waited for my name to be called. My sisters-in-waiting seemed to be mostly women in their forties and fifties—unsatisfied, just-divorced (I imagined) white women, some winding strands of yarn in lime green and chartreuse into intricate, interlocking knots with their trembling pale hands. No one made a sound. There was no television. Not even the annoying whisper of Muzak broke the tense silence.

Then a black lady walked in. My body tensed up when I realized that I knew her face. She was Ron Anderson's mom. Ron was a student at the college where I worked and, when he and his mom showed up in the college's counseling center together, the pair was known as THE Andersons—you said their name slowly, with doom, and hid from them if you could. They always came to see my coworker, Denise. She was the disability counselor and had known THE Andersons many years before I was hired. Ron was autistic. His mother was his stone-faced, fire-breathing advocate—until the fall semester of 2014. That's when Ron came to Denise's office and explained that he'd be dropping out of school to help care for his ailing mother. She had cancer. And there I sat, only six weeks after Ron's final visit to the counseling center, bearing witness to a now fireless dragon. She made her way up to the window and managed to eke out a smile at the nurse as she signed her name. Weakened, I imagined, by chemotherapy, her movements were sluggish. The hair left on her head circled her glowing scalp in thin wisps like skinny black cirrus clouds in a golden-brown sky. I said a silent prayer. For her and for me.

"Kristie?"

The calling of my name interrupted my astonishment and prayer. Buzzed through the door into another smaller, rectangular room, I sat in front of a lady in a cubicle and signed a barrage of paperwork, none of which I bothered to read. As soon as the last document was signed, I was buzzed through another door, this place becoming more like a luxurious maximum-security prison where they might send Oprah if she murdered Stedman. I entered another waiting room, this one larger, more square than rectangular. More middle-aged women, a few baby boomers, some even older, all in blue hospital gowns. I wondered how many thirty-four-year-olds they saw in this place. Probably not many. A nurse handed me a hospital band with my name on it and a gown to change into and directed me to one of the dressing rooms on the far end of the waiting area. I emerged from the dressing room and joined the waiting, aging women.

As I scanned the faces in the room—some fearful, some determined—I thought about the weeks that led up to my being in this place. I had called my closest friend, who is a nurse in North Carolina, to explain to her that I felt a sharp pain in my left breast, similar to the feeling of milk gathering for a newborn. Mimicking one of those horribly drawn clinic posters, I gave myself an exam. I felt a lump. "Are you sure it's a lump?" she asked. I was positive. She encouraged me to have someone else check and also to schedule an appointment with my doctor. The next morning, I stood nervously in the middle of Denise's office as her hand probed deliberately underneath my armpit, above my rib cage, and around my areola until, eureka, she detected it. A week later, I lay on my back in my doctor's office as she felt the mass and told me it might not be just fibrous tissue; it could be something worse. She sent me to the diagnostic center. "Just a precautionary measure," she said. Sitting in the glass building shocked my spirit. I scanned the room again and chose determination. Then a perky white woman in breast-cancer-pink scrubs called my name and another door opened.

Stretched out before me was a labyrinth of hardwood floors and halls adorned with muted, yet somehow encouraging, watercolor prints. I followed the perky woman into a bright white, sterile room with a giant machine in the center. This was the great fortune-telling machine; I pressed my breast against the icy glass, a camera took a picture, and the machine promised to tell me my fate. The perky woman tried to keep the mood light, making small talk. She mentioned the weather, asked if I had kids. I appreciated her effort but didn't say much. She took a look at my paperwork. "Your doctor wants an ultrasound as well. Let's get you set up for that."

I was hoisted off again to another place where I'd wait. This was the smallest space of all, no bigger than a closet or a handicap-accessible bathroom stall. It had a sliding door with frosted, beveled glass so no one could see in or out. There were about five chairs lining one side of the wall, a television mounted in the corner, and an end table with a Bible, a phone, and a box of Kleenex. Before I could begin to imagine the history of the tiny space—the heartache and secrets affixed to the wallpaper, the hard conversations suspended in the air, the moments taken, the breaths caught, the private pains, the worlds turned inside out, all packed tightly in this box of a room—the perky nurse came in to take me to get my ultrasound.

I lay down on the examination table. The room was dark in a soothing way. I zoned out while a nurse with curly almond-colored hair explained the procedure. "Blah, blah, blah . . . picture of the mass . . . blah, blah, blah . . . radiologist . . . blah, blah, blah . . . cold. Are you ready?" I nodded. The jellied probe roamed around my left breast as the nurse stared intently at the screen. Why was it always the left breast? The same breast that my mother had surgery on twice. The same breast that my grandaunt surrendered a year before she lost her life to breast cancer.

Once the nurse saw a clear picture of the mass, she told me to stay there while she consulted with the radiologist. I knew if she returned alone, I would be okay. If two people came back, everything would change. My mind strayed back to the withering Mrs. Anderson. My son is autistic, too. I know what it's like to live with that blue flame deep in your belly, ready to roar at a moment's notice at the slightest injustice, at the faintest whiff of mistreatment or prejudice. I always paraded around as though it were inextinguishable. Dragons were supposed to live for hundreds and hundreds of years, weren't they? I imagined God had plenty of reasons to punish me. But why punish my son? Why leave a disabled child motherless? Hadn't he suffered enough?

Just as the silence grew nearly unbearable, the almond-haired nurse returned. Alone.

VI

Not at all like a rag doll. The thought flashed through my mind as my head bounced off the carpet and I realized that I had forgotten about the concrete underneath. Lying on my living room floor, I thought I actually felt my cerebellum touch my skull, an awareness I never imagined. The saying goes something like, *He slung her around like a rag doll.* A lie. A rag doll is floppy and bloodless and lifeless. A rag doll doesn't bruise, heal, then bruise again. A rag doll doesn't marry the first man who asks and then allow him to eat her self-esteem for breakfast every day for the next six years. A rag doll doesn't grow lonely in her suburban fantasy and cut off all her hair and pick petty fights just to get her husband's attention, just to see if the cold heart in his chest will thaw. A rag doll doesn't first consider leaving, then think about cheating before ultimately landing on divorce. A rag doll doesn't swear and scream at the top of her lungs in front of her kids six months after the split that she still thinks is amicable just before he grabs her with a force she hadn't yet known existed, throws her to the floor, and pins her with his forearm as she writhes and thrashes and yells, "Get off of me! Get your fucking hands off of me!" until he realizes he's beating his son's mother in front him and frees her from his grip. A rag doll wouldn't ask God for strength as the ceiling fan stares down at her while she weighes the pros and cons of stabbing him versus calling the police before she chooses to just force him out the front door. And a rag doll wouldn't nurse a dull headache and bruised wrist for the next five days, silently suffering, too ashamed to tell. No. *Not at all like a rag doll.*

VII

When your parent is a crack addict, you grow accustomed to waiting for bad news, sometimes the worst news. You lie in bed awake at 3:00, 4:00, 5:00 a.m. because you don't want the phone call from a young sheriff's deputy or elderly coroner to startle you, the phone call saying they found your car, the one you haven't seen since payday, flipped in a ditch or on the side of the road two blocks down from a chop shop, relieved of its tires, radio, and speakers. Then the worst news. They found her in an alleyway, or in an abandoned crack house. OD. DOA. You won't cry because you've been bracing yourself for this since you were nine, when she was rushed to the emergency room for heart palpitations and you realized that she really could die. Your grandmother said it was the oxtails, but you saw the crack pipes, the pill bottles with holes burned in the sides, the razor blades and white lines. You hope that they do not ask you to identify her body when they call. You've seen the TV shows with the toe tags and cold naked bodies. The thought gives you the creeps. It's right about then that you hear the keys jingling in the lock, the creak of the door, the soft shuffling down the dark hallway, the familiar clanking of her silver bangles (she never leaves home without them wrapped around her wrist). You look at your clock: 5:42 a.m.

Lucky, I guess.

It didn't happen that way for us. There was no wee-hour phone call. No missing car. No overdose in a nefarious locale. No toe tag. It wasn't at all what I had been bracing for since I was nine.

She'd been clean and sober for several months, one of the longest stretches that I could remember. It was a particularly beautiful and crisp day, the same as how people remember 9/11 before the planes struck. I was dropping my son off at her house so that she could take him to summer school while I headed to work. It was our routine. I knocked first, then used my key and walked right in. She wasn't up yet. No TV on. No coffee brewing. No cigarette smoke. I poked my head into her bedroom. She was still in the bed. "Ma, we're here." No response. I walked over to her. I tapped her. I shook her. Nothing. I wanted to panic, but I couldn't. My six-year-old was watching me with his massive brown eyes. I felt like he could see everything, even what I was thinking. I dialed 911 and tried to quell the trembling in my voice, the lump growing in my throat. Everything from that point happened in a whirlwind. The 911 operator coached me through chest compressions. Within minutes, a cop came in. We moved her to the floor, and he continued CPR. Her pulse was faint, but it was there. I lied to my boy. "It's okay, baby. It's okay." But he knew. The EMTs burst in, and we rushed to the emergency room. The nurses peppered me with questions about her medical history and medications. I had remembered to grab her purse, so I gave her insurance card to the intake nurse. I called my supervisor and told her that I had to rush my mom to the ER. I called my husband and told him the same. A nurse ushered me and my son to a private waiting area. That fucking small, ominous room. The phone. The Bible. The Kleenex. A hospital security guard asked if she could take my son to get something from the gift shop. My husband walked in. I don't recall a conversation. Showing emotion wasn't his strong suit. Soon after that, a doctor walked in. His expression looked pained. The deep lines in his face—canyons crafted by years of carrying strangers' burdens. Silently, I began bargaining with God, praying for a debilitating stroke or some kind of coma. Before the doctor could complete an entire sentence, my husband grabbed me, an embrace that was one-half consolation and the other half literally trying to keep me from falling apart.

They let me see her alone. She lay on the stretcher in the middle of the room where they had worked to try and save her life. The words I said to her are secret even from me. Mostly, I just stared at her. Peaceful. Free from the addiction she had been trapped by for twenty-two of my twenty-six years. Free from the consequences of such a life—lost jobs, blown opportunities, failed attempts at rehab, relationships broken beyond repair. Finally free from all of it. I didn't know how to mourn my loss when I wanted to celebrate her freedom. I still don't. I ran my fingers through the silken gray hair that adorned her crown. A queen. I carefully slid those perpetual silver bangles from her right wrist, over her hand, into mine. My mother in front of me, lying on her back for the last time, as I stroked her temple, kissed her forehead, and invited her to slip back into that unknowable dark matter from which we all emerge. I understood then. Silence *is* God. And she was with Him, his eyes finally uncovered.

Quintonio's Lot

It must be what bright green moss or thin unbreathable air or the epitome of darkness or any other obscurity that one might find between that proverbial rock and a hard place feels like—pressed, paralyzed, flattened, suffocating, spread wide and thin, unrecognizable—to have to call the police on your son; to have to call the police on your black son; to have to call the police on your black son after you've seen Michael's lifeless body bronze in the Missouri heat, after you've seen Tamir struck down in the literal twinkling of an eye, after you've seen a brute in policeman's clothing hurl a black daughter across a classroom.

You are a native of two insane parallel universes. One world is draped in a dream where houses are neatly separated by white picket fences, and every Fourth of July smells like grilling meat and freedom, and the police are agents of virtue, bound to protect and serve. The other world is dripping in fear—no, rage—a roiling inner fire lit by a brutal history. The flames are fanned by habitual injustices. In this world the protectors and servers only know force. Their only language is composed of choke holds, gunshots, and electric volts of Tasers. To live simultaneously in both worlds is a terrible experiment in which you are the crazed subject— a perplexed lab rat. In one direction lies an unreachable fantasyland. In the other, a hellish reality from which there seems to be no escape. The maze is endless.

Shortly after the Newtown, Connecticut, school mass shooting in December 2012, writer Liza Long penned a powerful essay entitled "I Am Adam Lanza's Mother" in which she shared the story of her mentally ill son and called for solidarity with women like herself raising troubled children.

Long begins the essay by offering a moving description of her breaking point. During a tense morning commute with her agitated thirteen-year-old, she makes an abrupt turn, choosing to take her son to a mental hospital instead of school after he threatens to kill himself. As the essay continues, she reveals that hadn't been the first time her son had talked about suicide. She recounts a particularly disturbing episode in which he'd pulled a knife on her after she'd asked him to return an overdue library book. She ended up having to call the police and paramedics for assistance. As I read about the help she received from law enforcement, a small part of me envied Long. If she was Adam Lanza's mother, then I must be Quintonio LeGrier's mother.

According to *Chicago Tribune* reports, on Saturday, December 26, 2015, Chicago police fatally shot nineteen-year-old college student Quintonio LeGrier and his fifty-five-year-old neighbor Bettie Jones. LeGrier's father had called the police to report that his son had been threatening him with a baseball bat. The elder LeGrier asked his neighbor, Ms. Jones, to look out for the police while they waited for the arrival of help. Some relatives report that Quintonio had been struggling with mental illness in months leading up to that ominous December evening. When the police arrived, they opened fire, killing both Quintonio and Bettie. Quintonio did not have a gun. Nor did Bettie. Quintonio and Bettie were African Americans.

When I heard Quintonio's story, an uneasy breeze of familiarity blew cold through my bones. Just one week before Christmas 2015, on two separate occasions, I had wrestled my own fifteen-year-old son into the passenger seat of my Hyundai Sonata and had driven him to the downtown office of his developmental pediatrician, unannounced, after hours, because I didn't know what else to do. The first time we showed up I was stoic. The second time, I was in tears. My son has autism, and from the onset of puberty until he was sixteen years old, meltdowns had become more like genuine psychotic breaks—unpredictable, often violent, and always maddening for all involved. My life had become a string of constantly recurring episodes of airborne lamps and tablets, hours-long top-of-lung screaming sessions, phone calls from well-meaning but frazzled teachers, and late nights locked inside my own walk-in closet, coiled and crying on the floor, waiting for the veritable storm to pass. By the time Quintonio was killed, my son had completed his first full week of antipsychotic medication. Quintonio's fate still haunts me to this day.

Like Liza Long, I know the desperate isolation of living with a child who is a ticking bomb. Unlike Ms. Long, asking the police for help is hardly an option for me. Quintonio is the epitome of my worst nightmare, which plays out something like this: My son goes into crisis. I call 911. They arrive on the scene and, in six seconds flat, they see my son's dark skin, deem him a threat, fear for their own lives, and shoot him dead in his own home. And all I'm left with is a pool of warm red blood and an absurdly redundant story about how the cops killed my black boy. It's happened too many times to boys who bear a striking resemblance to my son, too many times for me to trust law enforcement, too many times for me to believe that calling them would result in anything but my son's dead body.

The citizens of Chicago protested the unlawful deaths of Quintonio and Bettie. It's an unfortunate, familiar process for hundreds of thousands of citizens of communities of color across the United States. Quintonio's parents joined the pitied ranks of childless mothers and fathers who lost their sons and daughters at the hands of police. *The Washington Post* reported that 994 people were killed by law enforcement in 2015. It is estimated that a quarter of those individuals showed some sign of mental illness based on data gathered from news reports, public records, official databases, and original reporting.

I wonder what Antonio LeGrier, Quintonio's father, must have been thinking during those hours and minutes leading up to what would turn out to be the end of Quintonio's short life. Did he hesitate before picking up his phone? Did he try to talk Quintonio down? Did he search Quintonio's frenzied face for the little boy he used to know, the baby he brought home from the hospital almost two decades before?

I have been dangerously close to Mr. LeGrier's crossroads on more than one occasion. When my son was fourteen, he had an acute meltdown that resulted in him running out of our house and pelting our garage door with rocks. The intermittent clanks and bangs grew louder, more violent, each rock launched with greater force than the last. This went on for about ten or eleven minutes. I pleaded with my son first before I began yelling and screaming. I was concerned about his deteriorating state of mind (as well as the deteriorating state of my garage door). But I was mainly consumed with the fear that a neighbor would soon call 911. As much as my son needed help in the middle of that crisis, no part of me could imagine a police officer of any race seeing my black son in that state and approaching him with measured compassion instead of a drawn weapon. We were fortunate that night. Most of the neighbors that lived within direct earshot had either not been at home or not cared enough to involve themselves by calling the police.

I also often wonder if LeGrier's parents were met with skepticism when they first suspected that Quintonio might have a mental illness. Were they ever told that mental illnesses were white people's conditions? How many times had they heard the phrase, *Ain't nothing wrong with that boy*?

When my son was first diagnosed at two years old, finding moral support from those who looked like me was a somewhat daunting task. My own grandmother had been highly critical, even questioning whether or not autism was a real condition. She went as far as to suggest that perhaps I'd allowed him to get a haircut too early and that's what caused his delays in development. She came from a time when racial oppression was palpable, direct, and seeped into every area of one's life—medical care included. Because her family couldn't often access quality medical care, they relied upon homespun solutions and their deep-rooted Christian faith. When these cures didn't work, it was often easier to pretend that the condition simply didn't exist. This was especially true with mental illnesses like schizophrenia and autism. Liza Long discusses the national stigma around mental illness in her essay. That stigma is twofold for my boy.

The compounded marginality of being black and having a mental illness or disability can be an astoundingly lonely place to live. Visits to church and to the barbershop—places where African Americans often find cultural validation and familial warmth—become rare and soon nonexistent after you grow tired of the whispers, side-eyes, and stares. The rejection stings at first, but after a while you learn to isolate yourself to avoid the pain. Once you come to terms with the idea that your child may never be fully accepted in their own community, you must still carry the water that all black parents must carry—preparing your child, no matter what their ability level, to thrive in a world where the color of their skin makes them a perpetual target.

As my son has gotten older and discovered a medication/therapy combination that works for him, the meltdowns have decreased dramatically. Instead of having one to two major episodes a week, he only has mild breaks occasionally, perhaps only one every six to eight weeks. While he manages his behaviors with more ease, he still is and always will be markedly different from the vast majority of the population. As he approaches adulthood, I think more and more about Quintonio. So far, my son has only had limited yet positive experiences with law enforcement (school resource officers, police presence at community events, TSA officers at the airport), but Quintonio's story is a stark reminder of how quickly everything can change. I still cannot honestly say that there is a circumstance in which I'd willingly call the police to help my son in a crisis. I thank God every day that passes without my having to face that decision.

Kristie Robin Johnson

Congratulations

Congratulations! You're the new parent of an endangered species. That's what I should've told him. Instead of sending the cute card adorned in the stereotypical baby blue with the face of an overzealous stork plastered on the front, I should've told him the truth. I should have taken the time to properly welcome him into the fold of angst-filled, red-eyed, frustrated parents of black boys. I should have told him what's it like to love something so fragile, a gift that could be taken at any moment for any reason at all—for talking to a girl whose skin is the wrong color, for playing his music too loud, for reaching to get his wallet, for looking too ominous, too suspect, too black. I should have told him that raising a black boy is an awesome endeavor fraught with a constant panic and a hovering rage. I should have explained that these first precious days of his tiny bronze prince's life may be his son's safest days indeed. I should have shared with him the pain of pouring your soul into raising a child only to realize that the stronger he becomes physically, the more vulnerable his black life becomes. I should've told him and his wife that when you devote yourself to a black man, a fully charged cell phone is not just a modern-day convenience, it is a necessity, it's camera sometimes the only bridge to justice in a corrupt system. I should have told the young and beautiful mother that loving her boy means always being on the ready—keeping dutiful watch over him as he plays in the sandbox when he's two years old, crossing her fingers every morning when she puts him on the bus at nine years old, nodding off to sleep with her phone held firm in her grip on the first night she lets him go to a party with his friends when he's fifteen, remaining in a state of perpetual prayer for his safe return. I should have explained to her that as her baby grows into a boy and then into a man, the nightmares will be piercing. I should have told her that it might not be a bad idea to keep a tailored black dress and a string of pearls in her wardrobe, just in case. I should have told them both that taking care of their young son will require a mastery of trickery and double-talk, because they are now tasked with convincing him that he is just as free as his white class-mates, teammates, and friends. I should have told them that they should probably take a shot of something strong before looking their boy in his brown eyes and telling a him the lie that this country is the greatest nation on Earth and that, if he works hard enough, he can do whatever he puts his mind to. I should have told my brother not to be startled when he picks up his son from school and suddenly finds himself gazing at the little white kids, with their stringy hair and pale skin, coveting their freedom, resenting their parents who will never have to stay up late at night think-ing of the right words to arm their sons with to prevent the police from killing them. I should have told him that those words, no matter how polite or grammatically correct, do not exist. I should've suggested that they consider disconnecting their cable and deleting their social media accounts before the broadcasted devastation becomes routine, before they can no longer be shocked. I should have told them both that the type of mental trauma that causes you to think to yourself, *Maybe we should just start drowning black boys at birth*, is inevitable—in essence, wishing our sons away. I should have told them that there is no escape. There isn't a zip code in America where their son's black skin doesn't put him in uninterrupted, imminent risk. I should've told my brother and his wife as they begin their young family that, along with love and pride, vigilance and paranoia will become cornerstones of their new existence. I wish I would've told him. Then, perhaps, I might not have received the text from him the week that Alton Sterling and Philando Castile were gunned down that simply read, "What the hell is going on? Twice in less than a week?"

I'm sorry little brother. I should've told you.

In Search of Heroes

The first Christmas that my son could write, his list for Santa read as follows: a purple wolf, boxing gloves, Power Rangers, and *his* superpowers. When he gave me the list, I reviewed it with amazement and a small dose of parental pride. I had managed to raise a child who, at only three years old, likened himself to Jesus Christ or Superman—having enough confidence to believe himself to be a demigod among mere earthlings. Looking at the world through his eyes and tethering myself to his unfettered imagination became my favorite pastime. Flying with him through alternate universes where he could be the world's richest Pokémon collector and the quarterback for the Denver Broncos and the youngest *American Ninja Warrior* champion all at once. Inspired by his natural loftiness and ostentatious self-esteem, my dreams became bigger, bolder. For a while, he seemed unstoppable. But even Superman had kryptonite. Even Jesus had the cross.

Something happened around the time he entered third grade. An awakening, an awareness, as if he'd taken a bite of forbidden fruit from the Tree of Knowledge of Good and Evil. He came home from school one day lamenting, "I hate my school." Not *I hate school* but *I hate my school*. Those four words triggered a tsunami of terrible in my brain. Statistics and research-based data began to run in a ticker tape across my consciousness: Governments predict the number of prison cells they will need based on third-grade standardized test scores. One in three African American males will be adjudicated in the criminal justice system at some point in their lives. Black boys are viewed as older and, therefore, less innocent than white boys. My heart palpitated at each thought.

Trying my best to quell the panic, I replied, "Baby, why do you say that?"

"There are no black people at my school."

"What are you talking about? There are lots of black kids at your school. And Latino kids and biracial kids. One of your classmates even has two mommies."

"I'm not talking about the kids. None of the teachers are black. The only black grown-ups are the custodians."

Speechless, I didn't know how to respond. His worldview was coming into focus, his eyes balked at the sight, and the blame belonged to me. In search of that elusive "better"—better schools, better homes, better neighborhoods—my husband and I chose to make our home in the suburbs long before our son was born. Like any parents, we wanted to give him the best opportunities possible. But almost a decade later, divorced and standing in the middle of my four-bedroom, two-and-a-half-bathroom, fenced-in, two-car-garage American Dream in a nice neighborhood in a highly ranked school district, I realized that in trying to provide the best life for my son, I had deprived him of something crucial—the opportunity to build a positive racial identity.

I and my degrees had not sufficed. His dad and his relentless work ethic had not been enough. His village, made up of black professionals, professors, and politicians, did little to combat the 180 days a year he spent immersed in an environment where all of the adults who looked like him—whose hair curled and lips plumped and skin tanned like his—were the help, the nameless, faceless ghosts who blended into the background like the dulling paint on the walls. Silent reminders of the odds he faces. In his own brown skin, he uncovered one of his greatest obstacles, the first nick in his tiny armor.

It is a pivotal question for the parents of African American children: How and when do you tell them the truth about their black lives? What words do you find while looking your beautiful and fragile brown sons and daughters in their eyes to tell them that they are, indeed, second-class citizens? How do you admit to them that the world isn't fair, the playing field not even? First, you let your heart break a little. Then you breathe. Then you decide whether you will teach them to pursue lives that are liberating and dangerous or lives that are polite and caged. For me the difference was between surviving and thriving. I preferred thriving, and I chose to teach my son liberty.

I have always reveled in the otherness of being black in America—never quite fitting in with the mainstream, having a twisted history that is one-half royal and one-half brute. I want my blackness to be explicit, dangerous, unforgivable. Like Nat Turner, Muhammad Ali, Sojourner Truth, Malcolm X, the members of N.W.A, Angela Davis, Marcus Garvey, Harriet Tubman, Jack Johnson, Huey Newton, James Baldwin, or any black person whose name elicits hundreds of thousands of tiny goosebumps on the otherwise smooth pink skin of white America. I want my boy to inhabit this same spirit, to not feel compelled to turn down his music, pull off his hoodie, refashion his hair, turn around his hat just to calm the fear and fury of a judging public.

But how?

Two weeks after my son declared that he hated his school, he came home with a social studies assignment about Frederick Douglass. He presented to me a brief four-paragraph passage with six comprehension questions on the opposite page. We began reading the passage in unison and I stopped after the second paragraph, where Mrs. Auld, one of Douglass's owners, had been described as "a kind lady" who had taught Douglass to read out of the pure goodness of her Baltimorean heart, as though owning another human being had been an inconsequential detail in an otherwise rosy story.

Once he'd completed the assignment, I asked my son, "What else do you know about Frederick Douglass?"

"Um," he began, "he's an a-boe-lishun-isth," pushing out the final syllable through his slowly returning two front teeth, deliberately choosing the hardest word that he could conjure to describe Douglass. His modus operandi has always been the path of most resistance. Even though he was nine, his voice rang with the syrupy simplicity of a six-year-old.

I smiled. "That's right. Did your teacher tell you that he wrote a book about his life?"

"No." He shook his head with a suspicious but intrigued expression.

"Well, he did."

I hopped up from the kitchen table and marched over to the bookshelf in the family room. Feeling smart and militant, I pulled the thin, inconspicuous spine from its home between bell hooks and Derrick Bell.

The slim paperback, though only thirteen years old, felt like an ancient rediscovery in my palms. As I thumbed through mushroom-colored pages—dog-eared and occasionally bleeding neon-blue highlighter from one page to the next—underlined passages and marginal handwritten notes in blue and black ink returned me to my twenty-three-year-old self, the determined college student reclaiming her opportunity, her pride, her life. I hadn't just read this book, I consumed it—dissected every sentence, picked apart Douglass's experiences, deconstructed and reconstructed every letter of every word. I had peeked from behind the stable as Frederick laid into Mr. Covey with a violence fueled by a life of savage oppression, stowed away in the shadows as Douglass finally liberated himself from the institution that still haunts the lives of his descendants centuries later. I returned to the table, book in hand, ready to right some wrongs—to correct the school's version of Douglass, of slavery, of America itself and my own mishandling of my son's black existence.

"*Narrative of the Life of Frederick Douglass,*" he read slowly, examining the text's age and use. "Can I take it to school? Maybe Ms. Dennis will let me read it to the class." His high-pitched voice chirped even higher, eyes shining with possibility.

"No, baby," I replied, careful not to dim the light of a brilliant idea. "I don't think your teacher would allow you guys to read it because of the language. It has some grown-up words in it." Grown-up words, not bad words.

One of the phrases that defined my childhood was my grandmother's *ain't no such thing as bad words.* Every time she uttered an angry *Shit!*, a sorrowful *Damn*, or the routine and often annoyed *Nigga please*, I was right there singing the traditional, "Oh, Granny, you said a baaad word!" She would always reply, "Baby, ain't no such thing as bad words. They're just grown-up words." Translation: they were words that she'd better not ever catch me using unless I was paying my own bills, in my own house, taking care of my own kids. I respected that. I like to think that my grandmother's refusal to brand a word as completely off-limits made me the lover of language that I am today.

"Why don't we read it together here at home, and you can tell Ms. Dennis what you're learning about Frederick Douglass?"

"Okay!"

And so we set off on a mildly ambitious course to read the short narrative (sixty-nine pages total) in one week. We took turns reading aloud right after bath time, just before going to bed.

And it is the wish of most masters within my knowledge to keep their slaves thus ignorant.

I love reading with my child. I love it not just because it allows me to savor a few precious intimate moments before puberty yanks him into the oblivion known as the teenage years; I love it particularly because reading didn't come to him with ease. Mastering kindergarten sight words had been rather tranquil, but when the time came to learn to sound out words, my son struggled tremendously. He'd be reading and come to a simple word like "cat." He'd make the correct sounds associated with the letters, "kuh-at." But when asked to blend the sounds to read the word, he'd say "tack." He seemed to be hearing the sounds in reverse. He started avoiding reading aloud whenever possible. Homework pained both of us. He'd stare down at the book or worksheet that he was studying, consumed by peril. His small chest would visibly rise then descend with stress. He'd begin to swallow laboriously, tasting anxiety with every deep gulp. You could almost see his mouth begin to dry, blood pressure surge. By the time he entered first grade, he'd been screened for dyslexia and placed in a small reading group for intensive instruction. The summer between first and second grade, I sent him to reading camp. It cost as much as two months' car notes, but the sacrifice paid off. He started to read on grade level by the end of the first grading period of second grade. We haven't looked back since.

When we snuggled on the sofa and began reading the Douglass narrative, the significance of the moment crystalized with a blinding light. We weren't supposed to be here, not he in his fire-engine-red fleece jammies nor I in my heather-gray oversized nightshirt, sitting comfortably on furniture that was ours, in a house that belonged to us, reading a book written by a fugitive. None of this was supposed to be. Throughout most of the antebellum South, indeed, right here in our home state of Georgia, it was against the law to teach a slave to read and write. As my child and I sat there mesmerized by Douglass's earliest memories—not knowing his own birthday, being abandoned by his grandmother, only seeing his mother on a handful of starry and cold nights when she could steal away to comfort him, remaining shoeless and without pants until eight or nine years of age—I fought back tears and thought, What a triumph. Me and my boy. Us just *being* there in that moment was both an anomaly and a victory. We continued reading through the end of the third chapter. Both of our eyes tired, we embraced.

"Good night, Mama."

"Good night, baby."

He dashed up the stairs as I closed the book, Douglass's ghostly matriarchs still haunting my soul.

It was a common saying, even among little white boys, that it was worth a half-cent to kill a "nigger," and a half-cent to bury one.

I stepped out of the bathroom to find my son already happily perched in the middle of my bed, thumbing through the pages of the inaugural selection of our impromptu book club, members to date: he and I. I climbed onto the queen-sized mattress and scooted next to him. "You ready?" I asked, gesturing for the book. No reply. His eyes cemented to the ivory pages, scanning and flipping at a maddening pace. After a moment, I realized that he hadn't morphed into some superhuman speed reader. He was looking—no, hunting—for cuss words. Grown-up words. I'd forgotten that I was reading with a nine-year-old boy, his existence filled with giggles and farts and boogers and burps. "Gimme that!" I demanded, snatching the book out of his hands.

"What?" he barely got out, just before bursting into a hundred belly laughs. I laughed with him. As it turned out, we would need the warmth of those chuckles to guard our hearts from Douglass's chilling account of plantation life.

We alternated reading aloud dense paragraphs composed of elegant and complex sentences. With erudite language and a truly eloquent voice, Frederick Douglass painted a world where disabled slaves were beaten mercilessly for years and eventually cast off the plantation to die alone in the thick of the forest because they were defective—the same way you or I would treat a broken shoe or a malfunctioning phone. He introduced us to slaves who literally ate scraps from a trough like hogs, their black faces rooting through Master's leftovers. He described in great detail the brutal, near-death beatings and the sheer barbarism of the slaveholders. A thirteen-year-old marginal note read: *Slavery dehumanizes the owners as much as, if not more than, it dehumanizes the slave.*

Midway through the sixth chapter, my son asked if we could take a break. I looked down at his face, his head leaning on my shoulder, eyes glassy and somber. His complexion had gone from its normal golden caramel tone to a faint pea green. Gripping his stomach, he announced, "I gotta go to the bathroom." Not really sure if he needed to throw up or cry or do both, I began to question myself. Why had I deemed it okay to allow a child to read such heavy content? Was he even emotionally mature enough to comprehend Douglass's struggles? Had I gone too far? I thought of a Flannery O'Connor quote taped to the shelves in my office: "To the hard of hearing you shout, and for the almost-blind you draw large and startling figures." This memoir was Douglass's bellowing voice and his large and startling figures. It occurred to me that sometimes when a person screams too closely into your ear, it can hurt. My son's eardrums were reverberating with the rhythm of an unforgiving cruelty. When he returned from the bathroom, I told him it was okay if he wanted to stop reading. He said he wanted to keep going. He was willing to soldier on. So that's what we did.

You have seen how a man was made a slave; you shall see how a slave was made a man.

Friday is barbershop day. And my kid relishes barbershop day. I always thought the thrill of the barbershop trip had been secondary to the simple fact that it was Friday, which meant staying up late, no tyrannical 6:00 a.m. wake-up call to *Get up and get ready for school!* and fresh pepperoni pizza washed down by ice-cold Mountain Dew. But when we began reading Douglass, I began to see the barbershop through my baby boy's eyes.

For him, the barbershop is a sanctuary bustling with brown and black faces of every station: the owner with his gap-toothed grin maneuvering his clippers with surgical precision; oversexed and underloved single mothers with toddlers in tow preparing for their first haircut; dope boys with gold teeth and golden hearts; young fathers in basketball shorts and expensive sneakers with their young sons, desperately trying to tear down stereotypes; professional dudes with neckties and dreadlocks and twenty-inch rims, getting fresh for the weekend; pastors, sometimes with Bibles in their hands, debating men who'd found Allah while doing six-year bids for possession with intent to sell; college kids in T-shirts with slogans like BLACK LIVES MATTER and HANDS UP DON'T SHOOT; and the occasional custodian dragging in for his usual fade after an honest day's work. In each sun-kissed expression, I imagine my son sees sixteen-year-old Frederick standing tall and invincible in the middle of Edward Covey's farmstead—part lion, part man—roaring the virtues of his manhood, his humanity, his right to breathe free.

On the Friday that we were reading Douglass, my son hopped in the chair and requested a mohawk, his declaration of independence. Later that evening as we read the final chapter, he cheered as our hero, our teacher, finally made it to New York and to freedom on September 3, 1838. Minutes later we both cheered the accomplishment of having finished the book.

The short drive from my house to my son's school was pregnant with something on the Monday after we finished the *Narrative of the Life of Frederick Douglass*. The sky still dark with remnants of night stretched out in front of us seemed to command quiet. I didn't even turn on the radio. As we turned into the parking lot, the silence was broken. "Mama, when I get to heaven I'm gonna ask Frederick why Mr. Hughes didn't tell on him when he beat up Mr. Covey!"

I smiled and nodded and replied, "You do that, baby." His energy lit up the black morning.

Reading the memoir didn't magically transform his white music teacher, PE coach, and principal into shiny new black educators, but it seemed to have confirmed in him a feeling that had resided deep down in his belly all along—that *he* was a hero. And every superhero has an origin story—a myth, a tale, a legend—some narrative that explains their extraordinary oddity, their superhuman strength, their enigmatic power. I think my son found his in Frederick's story. A black boy, just like him, fighting his way to a life that he was never meant to have. Beating all odds. Surpassing every miserable expectation. Born a slave, died free. As he gathered his backpack and jacket and rushed out of the car to his school's main entrance, I sang behind him, "I love you. Have a good day." He heard me but didn't turn around. Just before pulling off, I imagined a bright red cape catching the wind as he disappeared behind the double doors.

Kristie Robin Johnson

Homesick

I never realized, until I sat down and really thought about it, just how many myths exist about black life. *All black people are superior athletes. All black people are skilled dancers. All black women are perpetually angry.* What's even more astonishing is the rate at which we (and by *we* I mean black people) perpetuate and wholeheartedly believe some of these myths. One myth about black women that has followed me throughout my entire adulthood centers around black women in the workplace. It's been phrased a hundred different ways, but generally it goes something like this: black women are hard to work for and work with. From the moment I got my first job at eighteen years old in a posh department store in Atlanta's Buckhead neighborhood, I had been warned about the perils of working with black women and, especially, black female bosses and supervisors. I was told that black women (and sometimes women of all backgrounds) were catty and spread gossip and hated to see other women get ahead. And I was told this by other black women, including my own mother, grandmother, aunts, and cousins. Thankfully, I've been in the workforce long enough to know that they were wrong. Lately, I've been reminded just how false and harmful that myth can be.

As of late I've experienced a culture shock of sorts. I went from being a midlevel administrator in a heavily black, heavily female work environment to being a graduate student at a school with a heavily white student body and a heavily white workforce. On the first day, I came home feeling like my baby boy who once confessed that he hated his school because the only black adults were custodians or cafeteria workers or groundskeepers. He didn't see himself in leadership at all. I was beginning to understand how he felt. I was one of two black students in my day class, and the only one in my evening course. It was a few weeks before I saw any African

American professors. I was supposed to be relishing this time in my life. I was finally living out my purpose and pursuing my passion. I was supposed to be ecstatic and enjoying every minute of it. But most of the time I just felt homesick, even though I hadn't left my home.

I finally realized that I wasn't missing my physical home or my old job. I was missing *them*—those mythical black women that everyone had warned me about. For the preceding fifteen years, I had worked with and for a glorious array of African American women. Some were catty and a few were rampant gossips. I'd come across a tiny handful of haters. But most of these women were truly extraordinary. They took up money and baked cakes when you were ill. They sang songs and cracked jokes to make the time on the overnight shift pass more swiftly. They were generous and full of love and advice. The older ones believed it their duty to protect and educate the younger ones. The younger ones believed it their duty to respect and revere the older ones, often adding Miss or Auntie to the older ladies' first names.

I was lucky enough to build lasting friendships with a few of these women. And those bonds I missed the most. These were the women who listened painstakingly as I struggled to find out what was wrong with my child before he was eventually diagnosed with autism. Some of them wore unflattering champagne dresses in my wedding. They cried with me and brought food from Olive Garden and cussed out idiots when I didn't have the strength after my mother died. They sat with me and rummaged through my mother's belongings and missed her as much as I did. They babysat my new infant free of charge as my husband and I struggled to get on our feet. And when my marriage didn't work out, they didn't belittle me with *I told you so*. They comforted me when they could and prayed for me when they couldn't. They sprang into action when my son's summer camp called and said an ambulance was rushing him to the ER. One grabbed her purse as soon as I did. Another was on the horn with the camp director before I could get on the expressway. They always praised my achievements and never judged me when even I knew I was dead wrong. I missed their uproarious laughter, their unapologetic honesty, their tendency to care a little too much, their loving me in spite of myself.

As midterm approached, I was finally able to find enough time to grab lunch with my best girlfriends from my previous job. As we dined on soups, salads, and sandwiches and discussed everything from misshapen penises to the possible origins of Fetty Wap's injured eye, it occurred to me that something very sacred was happening amid our silliness. The tenderness that permeated the mood around the table was an energy I had not felt in a long time. It made us more than friends; it made us family. Our understanding and acceptance of one another built a near-impermeable connection. We didn't tolerate each other. We celebrated each other. Every day.

So, each day as I get ready for school, I pack up their prayers and well-wishes and indomitable spirits and put them in my bag right next to my books and laptop. And though I have no idea what the future holds for me, I do know that the next time I have the blessing of working alongside a fellow African American woman, I'll remember that woman is ultimately my sister, and I will treat her as such.

Dear Mary

I am sure that I am not the first to confess that your songs have been something of a therapeutic devotional guiding me through the peaks and valleys of my life. With ritualistic commitment I put "Share My World" on repeat every time I think I've fallen in love. "Take Me as I Am" fueled my bounce back after my divorce. I sang every single word of "Reminisce" from memory the morning after I fell back into the arms of an old flame, and "Doubt" has been my anthem since I found the guts to take a chance on myself and follow my passion. So when I heard that you were coming to my hometown, I had to get a ticket. And with a little luck and some favor from on high, I was blessed to be on the very front row with my best friend as you surpassed every expectation.

You were beyond amazing. You did not put on a show. You did not perform. You provided an experience—spiritual, organic, feminist, magnetic.

You proved a point. You don't need dancers, pyrotechnics, wind blowers, cherry pickers, feigned dramatics, risky entrances from the rafters or trap doors, or elaborate stage setups to give people their money's worth. With just your world-class band, three heaven-throated backup singers, strategic lighting, and a video screen, you gave us something priceless—you gave us *you*. All of you. From the moment you appeared with that wicked platinum-blonde bob, your presence took over the arena and spilled into the entirety of the crowd in waves of joy, pain, and truth. "Just Fine" boomed through us, giving life to the dead and courage to the living. We cheered you on as you took us back to our youth. *We* sang "Sweet Thing" to *you*. Your voice found a gorgeous gospel rasp when you revisited "Not Gon' Cry" and a Holy Ghost pull took us captive by the end of "No More Drama" when you literally lay your body down on the stage.

Breathtaking. I am sure that the well-to-do white couple sitting next to me must have wondered what awesome witchcraft was commencing. They were privileged to bear witness to the beautiful sorcery of soul. It happens when we gather and the mass breathes as one, moves as one, wails as one, shouts as one, and believes as one. Mary, we believed in you and with you. And when you asked for the lights to be lifted so that you could see the faces of the enraptured throng, your face softened. Your smile was genuine, your amazement honest. You were instantly endeared to the many thousands of black, white, brown, yellow, and red Augustans gathered to see you. The hypnosis was both complete and mutual.

I tell you all this to simply say, Thank you. Thank you for "Real Love" and jerseys and baseball caps. Thank you for *My Life* and *Share My World* ushering in my womanhood. Thank you for the wealth of brilliance that you've collected in your recordings. Thank you for putting your living, longing, and suffering into your voice and then bellowing them out into the world from the very center of yourself like the brave, militant flower that you are.

I left liberated and filled where once I was empty.

Love and admiration,
Kristie Robin

Other

It isn't normal for your first thought after sex to be of your mother. Normal people roll over and go to sleep. In my younger days, I would roll a blunt if the mood was right. My best friend once confessed that if the sex is really good, she cleans her whole house. Tonight is different. The sex was amazing and long overdue. But staring up at the ceiling of my bedroom, the walnut canopy creating a perfect rectangle to frame my placid and naked limbs, I keep seeing the fiery face of my mother. Her face is an unshakeable reminder that the man who just lifted himself from my body and my sheets and stumbled across the dimly lit room to my bathroom is another woman's husband.

I study his silhouette, remembering the tall, gaunt teenager I once knew. I wonder how he came to be this complicated and sculpted shadow standing nude in my bathroom.

It was his slight frame and eternal youth that made me happy as a young woman. His smile—no, his grin—that crinkled the bridge of his nose when it appeared burst with gregariousness and warmth. It was as if he lived on the verge of laughing out loud. He was humble and sunny and safe. I loved him back then because he was courteous and uncomplicated. As an eighteen-year-old girl on my own in a big city, most men were predatory creatures, sharpened by edges I had yet to experience. He was different. He was sweet. He loved his mother. He was still polite. We dated briefly, off and on, in our late teens and early twenties, when we didn't know that life is more gray than black-and-white, before we understood the strange musings of our elderly kin, before we would learn that sometimes there exists no difference between loving and demolishing a person.

We rediscovered each other in the most unoriginal manner. We reconnected online—Facebook to be exact. In a way, this could all be

Mark Zuckerberg's fault, with his inherent genius and profound understanding that humans, at our most primitive, seek attention. We all just want to be seen, noticed, liked. I'm a firm believer that if a person really wants to reestablish a connection with someone, they'll do the work. They'll reach out to your mom in your hometown. They'll ask mutual friends about your whereabouts. Even though the site is called Facebook, no one there really wants to see your face. They are just willing to offer a few moments of contrived attention in hopes that you will do the same for them. A true nonconformist, I didn't even join Facebook until 2014 when I succumbed to peer pressure, and I felt silly when I did so. My old friend (the naked man in my bathroom) inboxed me literally within minutes of me establishing my page. He asked the standard long time, no see questions: How are you doing? How are your kids? Husband? Job? I replied to each question immediately with an unconscious smile and equally standard answers: I am doing well. The oldest is heading to high school and the baby is playing football. The husband is fine, still selling cars. I've been at the technical college for two years now. The husband part was a lie. I'd recently filed for divorce, but I had not yet learned how to articulate the splitting of my family. I ended the conversation abruptly, explaining that I was about to step into a meeting, and said that I'd catch up with him later. I didn't. We wouldn't speak for months.

The following summer came early and without warning, as it always does in Georgia, and by the time the summer semester began at the college, my students had already been sporting short-shorts, halter tops, flip-flops, and wifebeaters for four or five weeks. The summer term always signaled a collective laziness on campus. Fewer students, fewer lines, fewer frustrations. I had enough free time to pick up the local black paper and thumb through it. It was delivered to the college every Thursday morning. As I turned the pages, glancing at ads for black-owned insurance agencies, law firms, and a dentistry practice, I saw it. That bright adolescent grin from my past. It was a typical headshot—white shirt, blue suit, yellow tie. He was featured in a professional profile, having been named the CEO of a popular annual expo. Looking back, I am not sure whether it was the premature heat, the quick jolt of emotion I felt when I saw the picture, or the simple idleness of that particular day, but something made me believe that it would be a good idea to send him a congratulatory instant message via Facebook.

He responded faster than I expected. It was as if he had been sitting there for a hundred days, frozen in time, waiting for the message. My phone lit up within seconds of hitting the send button. "Thank you. How are you doing?" We did the same song and dance, except this time I was sincere about catching up and I sent my number in the reply. Again, I got a text message on my phone in less than a minute. I was titillated by the surge of attention. He lived about an hour away, so I asked him how often he comes to town. He said he'd be in town that night for a basketball game the next day. His next text was a request to call me. Already cognizant of the fact that I was way too eager, I said, "Sure," and waited for my phone to ring.

"Hey!" I answered, struggling to find just the right balance between delight and aloofness.

"Oh my God! It's so good to talk to you," he gushed. "First, let me say that you look great. You haven't changed a bit. I saw you somewhere. You were speaking?"

"Yeah, probably an event for the school. Thank you. So, I see that you're still in the honeymoon stage. That's really cool." I was referencing recent pictures of him and his wife posted on social media. Photos of vacations, gifts, romantic dinners—all of the mushy stuff that made my freshly divorced stomach churn. He had married around the same time that my marriage was near its end.

"I just post those to keep people out of my business. You know what I mean?"

I was stunned and silent. I didn't know what he meant. Even on the best days of my marriage, I never felt the need to post pictures to prove our happiness to anybody. I was never that self-conscious.

He ignored my silence and continued, "You know me. I can't sit still. I'm ambitious. We've always been equally yoked. You get me. Right?"

"Yeah, I understand. You have always been a Jamaican—with your seventeen damned jobs!" We both laughed. It was an inside joke. For better or worse, he was always an opportunist. He's 75 percent work horse and 25 percent show horse. He chases dreams relentlessly, often to his own chagrin. It's always been a part of his appeal.

The conversation continued for about five more minutes until he got another call. He told me he'd call back. He did, sort of. He sent a text message shortly after I left work that day. We texted back and forth deep into the evening like two teenagers—exchanging flirty jokes filled with innuendo, LOLs, and smiley faces. I ended up inviting him over for drinks. I wanted to see him, and I didn't want to drink alone. Again. Just as he had all day, he obliged. By 9:30, he was at my home.

I opened the door feeling giddy and ridiculous, and then feeling stupid because I felt giddy and ridiculous. He was handsome, no longer cute. Our hug was tight and genuine. It was the same hug you give a relative you actually like when you haven't seen them in months. We settled into my couch comfortably. He sipped scotch and I drank beer. The conversation was easy and relaxing. I'd forgotten that I was capable of having that type of rapport with a man. It was evident as soon as he walked in that he, like most folks our age, was inseparable from his phone. He apologized for glancing at it while we talked. It was clear that someone was trying to reach him.

About an hour into our reunion, he looked at his phone one last time and then confessed with a certain exasperation, "Shit! I gotta go." He wanted to destroy that contraption. I was disappointed, even though I shouldn't have felt that way. When I stood to walk him out, a sense of tangible urgency filled the room. And both of us were drawn to it like a three-year-old staring at a perfectly iced cake on her birthday just before the candles are lit and the obligatory song is sung, dying to get it all over with and just taste the cake, the seduction almost unbearable.

Our goodbye embrace started like the hello embrace, my arms reaching up around his neck, his arms reaching down around my waist. But he pulled me in so much closer, pressing his heat against mine. Before I could think about anything—his wife, his kids, his job, his dreams, his intentions—I pulled his face to mine, breathed him in like the first spring morning, and we kissed. It was then that I realized I'd been chasing *that* exact kiss for the last eleven years. He gave his hands license, then mine. He took my hand and pushed it from his neck following a path down past his chest and belly button to his belt buckle then zipper to feel him stiffen. He wanted me to know that he knew how I thirsted for this warmth. He knew I'd been married too long and had become discontented with Friday-night missionary and the occasional Sunday-morning fellatio. He knew that it was his virility I imagined to get me through those mundane marital episodes. He knew that my husband, literally, had not put his tongue in my mouth since our wedding night. He knew my misery. He knew me.

His phone buzzed again. We pulled apart slow and smiling. He sighed and then whispered again with great disappointment, "I gotta go."

I whispered, "Don't be a stranger," and walked him to the door. I was relieved that he had to leave. I wasn't ready to become that dreaded other—the woman that all women hate. The home-wrecker, the whore, the side chick, the jump-off, the mistress. I wasn't ready to be judged like that, or even worse, to judge myself in that way. But while I wasn't ready that night, I went to bed certain I'd see him again. We continued to communicate, and two weeks later he messaged me saying he'd be back in town on Tuesday.

It was his radiance that lured me when I first knew him. Now, so many years later, it would be his darkness that would draw me near. It was his new coolness and shrewdness and selfishness that brought him to my doorstep and eventually up the stairs.

He made me feel like a Jill Scott song—explosively feminine, brilliant, and tender. He made me remember parts of my body that I had long forgotten—the small of my back, the silken half-moon behind my ear, the soft insides of my knees, and the glorious curve of my sun-kissed shoulder. He even remembered the pink, translucent skin in the webs of my fingers and graciously rested his fingers in between. We laughed out loud and kissed each other's lips as though we belonged to one another, as though this were not a forbidden entanglement.

I am supposed to feel guilty. I am prepared to feel guilty. I thought that my Southern Pentecostal upbringing had stuffed my conscience with enough fire and brimstone to create a mountain of culpability. But I lie here, not feeling much except my mother's piercing eyes.

I'm surprised by my own blameless demeanor. But I shouldn't be shocked at all. Half of all marriages end in divorce. My spouse and I have already gone our separate ways, divorced for several months. His relationship is clearly dangling in the balance. A long time ago, I taught myself to believe that a marriage was a sacred thing of beauty, and the absence of infidelity made it all the more holy, and I held tight to this expectation in spite of my environment, not because of it.

The only serious relationships that my mother or grandmother had during my formative years were with married men. Infidelity was such a regular occurrence in my world that when I first introduced my now ex-husband to my family, my grandmother's sister ever so discreetly, yet casually, pulled me to the side and asked if he was married. This lack of committed love made me judgmental of their callousness. The extramarital affair did not look appetizing. The lives of "other women" seemed to be filled with only waiting and dissatisfaction. Very little joy, almost no fulfillment.

We never addressed my grandmother's lover by his first name. It was always Mister. Though their relationship was disreputable, they both carried themselves with an ancient dignity, as though they had risen directly from the sands where pharaohs were buried. They saw each other regularly for more than two decades. Then in a sad and serendipitous twist of fate, Mister's wife passed away just as my grandmother began to grow ill. They had the two years before my grandmother died to enjoy an unfettered love. It was as if God were rewarding their uncanny ability to conduct their affair with some decency. I could never be sure, but I think that my grandmother was the happiest she'd been in her life during those last months with him. He was so well respected and admired by the family that we included him in her obituary and invited him to walk with us in the funeral procession behind her frail and solemn body.

If my grandmother's relationship represented the best possibilities of a union with such tainted beginnings, then my mother's relationships represented everything else. My father was already married when he met my mother. She would describe the encounter as love at first sight and I would roll my eyes. Theirs was a connection marked by equal parts passion and tumult, with not an ounce of boredom. Eventually my father left his wife, married my mother, and gave her me. After my father died when I was just four years old, my mother retreated into a courtship with a man from her past. He, too, was married, and we addressed him by his first name. For the next twenty years, I was the innocent bystander struck by their multiple breakups and makeups, my mom's deep depressions and tears, her lover's frustrations. When Mama was angriest with him, she'd refer to him as "that black bastard." I used to think she meant black as in his skin; but now, I'm pretty sure that she meant black as in his heart.

In the midst of their man-made hurricane, my mother died. It was sudden, in her sleep, in the summertime. I was moved by the depth of his suffering. The day after she died, I answered my phone and was met with the most awful sound. A pent-up agony leapt from the other end of the phone. I recognized the broken voice of my mother's longtime companion. I made out a breathy whisper, "I . . . I can't turn the corner." For several years before, at least three times a week, he had made the brief trek from his home to my mother's apartment. But today, the darkest of days, he just could not bring himself to turn down the winding road that used to lead inevitably to her. I met him at the corner or, I should say, I met what was left of him. For the first time in my life, I witnessed masculinity at its breaking point—uncovered, defenseless, soundly defeated. With tears streaming and hands shaking, he pulled six hundred dollars in cash out of his pocket and placed it in my hands. He asked that we play a certain song at her service. He said that she always liked it. He said that he could not come to the memorial because the pain was too great and asked me to forgive him. I thanked him, forgave him, and agreed to add "Fully Committed" to the funeral program.

As I drove back to my mom's tiny apartment, by then spilling over with seldom-seen cousins who were more nosy than compassionate and four or five genuinely concerned friends, I wondered if she'd seen him from the beyond, falling apart in broad daylight over her dead body. I wondered if she ever knew, really knew, how much he loved her. He stayed in touch and still calls on occasion to check on me and my children. I often imagine that we—he and I—rush to sleep each night with the same lingering hope to see her in our dreams.

I wanted this sin to pass me by. I wanted to prove that I was greater than temptation and loneliness, to prove that I was superhuman, void of any sign of weakness. I foolishly wanted to somehow be more than the women who bore me. It is popular to lay the blame for unfaithfulness at the feet of sources outside yourself. My husband works too much. My wife is frigid. He was mine first. Any excuse will suffice. No one ever says that they were just curious or horny or both. Many will admit that they were weak but fall short of admitting that they were gratified by the act. So when this sin visited me, I prayed to be impervious and not to praise his wide grin when he called. In the beginning, we pretended to be more interested in each other's journeys than the palpable spell that filled the space between our pauses. Soon we stopped pretending. We were not twenty and star-crossed. We were much older and overwhelmed. He was not Superman. I was not Wonder Woman. We were humans being human.

Still catching my breath as he turns the knob on the shower to wash me away, I wonder, What if I am truly my grandmother's granddaughter and my mother's daughter? What if I, too, am destined to be outlived by my greatest transgression? What would happen if I met my demise tomorrow? I imagine that he would get the news secondhand, in a text message or Facebook post. I imagine him not being able to mourn me inside his home—their home. He would have to go outside, as if I was some disgusting, unhealthy habit he had sworn off but just couldn't seem to kick. Perhaps he would escape to the patio or maybe he'd just sit in his car in the driveway. I imagine him placing his face in his hands and weeping silently or not at all. Who would he tell? Who could he tell? Who would understand a cheater's grief? I imagine he would have no refuge and would be left to bottle up his pain and bury all his memories of me in the dark, uncharted part of his subconscious. I wonder if he'd even consider turning the corner to offer my children his condolences for the loss of a woman he had loved both too much and not enough.

In the middle of daydreaming, it occurs to me that he is a total stranger. He reminds me of the strange house I pass each day on my way to work. It sits in the absolute middle of nowhere on a less-traveled back road, a beautiful brick home with columns on the porch. It's the kind of structure one might find on the cover of *House Beautiful* or *Southern Living* or any other interior decorator's magazine filled with furnishings and trinkets that most of us could not afford. From the road, the house is a magnificent mystery. The yard is not just fenced in; it is gated by iron bars and razor wire. On sunny days, the reflection from the wire is near blinding when I come around the curve before the house comes into view. I have always wondered what terrible intrusion or invasion could have occurred out here, miles and miles away from urban conveniences and urban hazards, to leave the owner with no choice but to put up this brutal barrier between them and the world. I gaze at my lover with the same curiosity. Who or what had betrayed him in such a way to leave him so brazen and cold enough to stray? This isn't the man I used to know. Perhaps he is a sharpened predator like all the rest, and his secrets are his and his alone.

I feel like Eve in Eden. All at once, I notice my bareness and weakness, and I am frightened by it. I can hear my mother's posthumous voice saying, *What the fuck are you doing? Girl, you need to run like hell!*

My reply to her dead, undead voice is, *If you ran like hell from my daddy, I wouldn't even exist!* But her rightness is inescapable. Almost as inescapable as the lure of offering my body to this married man. Offering it to be soothed, to be praised, to be judged, to be preyed upon, to be discarded. The scent of Dove body wash starts to fill the room, reminding me that he'll be leaving shortly, and I'll be single again in a matter of minutes.

I watch him dress, re-covering his desert-colored skin, a hint of gold underneath. I set aside my thoughts and pull on my robe. I walk him back down the stairs and to the door, where his entrance gave me butterflies and his exit will leave me undone. We kiss again. Like a couple. There's that grin. He pulls out of my driveway and disappears down the street. A strange house, returning to his real life, behind a razor-wire fence on a forgotten road, in the middle of nowhere. As I head back up the stairs weightless, I hear my mother's presumptuous tone: *You love that nigga, don't you?* Gone from the Earth for almost nine years and she still manages to annoy me by asking me questions to which she already knows the answers. Again, she's right. I think I do love him. Maybe I never stopped.

In that moment, I make a terrible, conscious, grown-up decision that I'd rather be somebody's other than nobody's nothing. The only thing worse is being somebody's nothing. And I had my fill of that role while I was married. My husband had been twenty-five years older and almost completely devoid of emotion. Early in our marriage, he had declared that I needed to "learn how to be a wife." On more than a few occasions, I cooked dinner before he got home from work, because that's what wives were supposed to do, and when he didn't like what I cooked, he threw the plate in the garbage. In the ten years that we were together, he brought me flowers exactly one time. He didn't cry when my mother died or bother to get a decent suit to wear to her funeral. I had the type of marriage that did not turn me against men; it turned me against the institution. And when I became tired enough and brave enough, I left. "Other" from this vantage point starts to look better and better. Maybe my mom and grandma came to this conclusion too. I wish I could ask them.

So that scarlet O belongs to me now. I follow the rules and I wait. I wait for his texts, his calls, his IMs. I do not call him in the middle of the night or at dinnertime or on Sundays. He's memorized my schedule. He knows when I'm at work and when I'm at home alone. He knows which weekends my kids are with my ex-husband. Some weeknights he slips in after they are asleep and slips out before they wake with the sun. A thief. When we are together, we never discuss his wife or family. Ever. Sometimes we talk about my oldest son. He remembers him from the early years. But we never talk about my youngest boy, who came after I got married. We don't talk about divorce, not even my own. We don't talk much at all. We fuck. We make love. We sleep. Not always in the same order. Every three weeks or so, some random song or a sting of religious fervor inspires me to give him up and straighten out my life. Then two days later, he calls, and I can't stop my heart from fluttering. I can't stop my facial muscles from contorting into a giant smile. I can't stop the fever between my thighs from spreading all over. We've managed to invent a tiny universe, all our own, pieced together with stolen minutes and hours, useless memories, sex, and secrecy. And I hurtle through it, willing and aimless—an inhabitant of planet other.

American Mourning

I glance down at my phone. There are two missed calls from Denise. Denise never calls this early. Text? Maybe. But an actual call? Never. She knows I'm only a few minutes away from the office. I'll see her in a matter of seconds. I immediately wonder what's wrong. I fumble at the last red light before turning into the parking lot while trying to call her back. Her phone rings once. She answers. No "Good morning," just a rushed, "Is Bobby okay?" The question throws me off. Bobby is my oldest son. I'd put him on the bus around 6:30 this morning. He's a freshman in high school, and school just started two days ago. I reply to Denise, "He's fine. He's at school. Have you heard something?" She tells me that her mom, who works for a neighboring school district, heard that Bobby's school is on lockdown this morning.

Lockdown. The word gives me pause. Lockdown is a term that has evolved in the modern lexicon. When I was a little girl, we only associated lockdown with prison culture. You thought of bright orange jumpsuits, maybe stripes. You thought three hots and a cot, and Attica, and Rikers Island. Today lockdown might be the most dreaded two-syllable word imaginable to American parents. Images of Columbine, Virginia Tech, and Newtown flood the mind. The vision of terrified, grief-stricken teenagers rushing across a campus, single file, hands on heads, flashes in front of you. You remember a sitting president in tears. You remember surviving parents' tales of leaving hollowed-out schoolhouses childless. You desperately try not to remember.

My own school, George P. Butler Comprehensive High School, had been one where the margins met the middle, buzzing with kids from all walks: kids who sold drugs, kids who did drugs, kids who'd never seen their incarcerated dads, kids whose parents owned businesses and drove nice cars, kids who'd never consumed anything harder than an Arnold Palmer. By the time my sophomore year began, we had to file through metal detectors before entering the hallways. After graduation, some of us went to college, many of us went straight to work, a few of us went to jail.

I don't recall being afraid. I do remember feeling annoyed—at the inconvenience; at the hovering sense of violation as police waved wands across your face, torso, knees; at the judgment that the wands and cops and metal detectors and German shepherds represented. No one ever got shot at Butler High. It was just assumed that because violence was a regular occurrence in some of our neighborhoods, the mayhem would eventually bleed into the school.

Two years after my graduation, a new kind of terror rocked us all as live television broadcasts delivered the events that were unfolding in Littleton, Colorado, right into our homes, into our chests. I remember wondering, *Where are their metal detectors, wands, and dogs?* Years passed, and school shootings became eerily commonplace and somewhat predictable. At schools like Butler, if a student is shot, it is most likely an act of retaliation aimed at a specific student or group of students—a drug deal gone bad, revenge for some wrongdoing, a personal beef gone too far. Shootings at schools like Columbine, though— gleaming modern buildings situated in the heart of suburbia, constructed with above-median-income taxpayer dollars, packed primarily with white kids from the middle (very few from the margins)—are random and most often driven by the psychological underpinnings of being an outsider in a universe of wannabes and look-alikes.

Bobby's school is more Columbine, less Butler.

8:41 a.m.

I tell Denise that I'll see her when I walk in. I take a moment to breathe and collect myself. I send a text message to my son's teacher, knowing full well that if they are, indeed, on lockdown, she will not be able to respond. But I can't do nothing. Nervously, I type, *Is everything okay?* It's all my fingers can muster. I pray for a quick reply.

No reply. My heart sinks a little. It takes the forceful intention of every cell in my body to lift myself out of my car and march into my office without shaking so violently that I drop my coffee cup on the asphalt. I put on my best Bobby's-all-right face and walk my fiercest Bobby's-all-right walk. I figure, if I act like Bobby is all right and look like Bobby is all right, then, goddamn it, Bobby is all right.

Once in my office, I begin furiously attempting to access the school's website to no avail. This creates one of the strangest emotions I've ever felt—fear with a single vein of comfort pumping right through it. This confirms that the school is, more likely than not, on a lockdown. This also means that I'm not experiencing this unsettling groove in the pit of my belly alone. Hundreds of other parents are just as on edge. A Google search of my son's high school turns up a photograph on a local news website of multiple police cars lined up at the front entrance. There's that sinking feeling again.

The image takes me back to one week earlier. I pulled up to Lakeside High School with my two boys and met a sea of cars, SUVs, pickup trucks, middle-aged moms, midcareer dads, a massive throng of teenagers (some gangly, some awkward, some perfect), and teachers and staff replete with fake smiles and forced cheer. Bobby has autism, and crowds have always unnerved him. I had considered not taking him to his first high school open house but decided against it at the last minute. He'd have to learn to conquer his anxieties at some point.

When we finally found a parking space, Bobby refused to get out of the car. He was afraid. *Patience*, I whispered under my breath. I told Bobby that his little brother and I would be right there with him. I told him that a lot of kids were nervous. He still wouldn't budge. Determined to attend this open house, I called my ex-husband, who was stuck at work. He tried coaxing Bobby and it seemed to be effective. Bobby finally emerged from the car. As we approached the main entrance, he clutched my wrist so tight, I felt the small half-moon indentations forming in my skin from the grip of his nails. Then I felt an abrupt jerk when Bobby bolted towards the woods adjacent to the school as we approached the double doors—those very same double doors that are staring back at me from the computer screen right now. God knows what lies behind those doors. I can't help but think that he might have been right to retreat. Those woods seem to hold an odd solace now.

With the aid of two Columbia County police officers, Bobby did eventually go into the open house. He met his teachers and briefly toured the classrooms. It hadn't been without spectacle, but our goal had been achieved. I wonder if one of those officers is there this morning. I wonder if he remembers the terrified, lanky black boy with big eyes and an inelegant gait.

Denise is trying to preoccupy me with inane small talk while I try my best to pretend to be unaffected. Bobby *is* all right. I will the words in my brain over and over again like a mantra. I see reports that pictures on social media show teenaged boys with firearms in and around the school property.

So, this is us now? It occurs to me that maybe I'm not pretending at all. Maybe I really am unaffected. Maybe this is what we can expect from morning in America now. Perhaps it is too much to ask that kids go to school without a constant lump in their throats, tremor in their hands, dent in their hearts. Perhaps we're all numb, even Bobby and his classmates. After all, they are the generation that watched the twin towers, packed with panicked New Yorkers, burn and then tumble to the ground before they could talk. My youngest son saw other first graders like him go to a school not much different from his and never return home. They're cold and don't even know it. Their young hearts are encased in a thick ice, solidified by reports of daily, monotonous violence. The words "lockdown" and "massacre" and "active shooter" have become a part of their zeitgeist. This is us now.

10:29 a.m.

Finally, I get a robocall call from Lakeside High School. The principal's voice is deliberately casual. He explains that the school had only been on a soft lockdown and that the suspects were not students at the school, that they had been arrested, and that no weapons were found on the school property. Bobby probably hasn't a clue about the threats or the Facebook posts or the dread that's been eating me alive for the last two hours. He is all right.

*

3:44 p.m.

Bobby gets off the bus, and I hug him for the first time in a long time. I hug him so long he begins to think it weird. I pull back and let him get on with his afternoon—snacks, homework, the usual. A few minutes later, his younger brother walks in, and I hug him too long as well. He asks if I'm okay. I tell him I'm fine. I admire my sons, their resolve, their ability to live in this madness.

The collective sigh of relief that befalls the entire community is palpable and telling. We'd literally dodged a bullet. We were grateful, but soon forgot, and, just like the majestic Savannah River that borders us, the news cycle rolled on. We went back to our routines—our morning coffees, our 8:00 a.m. commutes, our football practices, our soccer games, our mundane conversations about dinner and coupons, our less-than-titillating weekend sex, our car washes and bake sales—as if nothing had ever happened, as if we hadn't all been pacing back and forth, wringing our hands, checking our phones, praying for our kids, just a few days ago. We'd given more attention to fender benders. We barely slowed down to notice our normal shifting from gray to black. Nothing to see here. Just another American morning.

Kristie Robin Johnson

Low Country Lamentation

It was supposed to have been a typical summer vacation marked with ocean views, fresh seafood, adult beverages with exotic names, an abundance of sun, and an even greater abundance of laughter. My close friend and I had planned the getaway for more than a month—a weekend trip to charming Charleston, South Carolina. The week prior to our scheduled jaunt changed everything. The previous Wednesday, a demented white supremacist traveled more than a hundred miles to murder nine black worshippers at the historic Emanuel African Methodist Episcopal Church (known as Mother Emanuel), located in the heart of Charleston. Our first inclination had been to pray, then to cry, but we never thought to cancel the trip. Perhaps travelers who hadn't been raised in the South would've thought twice—vacationers who didn't grow up in counties named for slave owners, who weren't accustomed to the frequent sight of breeze-caught Confederate flags swaying from the backs of pickup trucks and grandmothers' porches, who hadn't learned to tuck away inconvenient histories that included black churches reduced to rubble and charred bodies swinging from pecan trees. Since this had been the entirety of our existence, the tragedy, for us, was more disappointment than shock. So, we packed our bags, kept our reservations.

Reality was inescapable as we were greeted by the Crowne Plaza's flags hovering at a miserable half-staff. It was a reminder that this trip would encompass more than simple revelry and relaxation; it would include an exercise in collective suffering and compassion like we'd never experienced in our lives. Friday evening was steamy and sticky, the kind of heat that could only be tolerated, not enjoyed, on a vacation. My friend and I had come to the conclusion at some point while traveling on I-26 that we'd need to visit Mother Emanuel. We agreed that to do otherwise would have been blasphemy. Our own grandmothers, who had survived the indignity of segregation and the daily threat of violence against black bodies, would have wanted this experience to remind us not to get too comfortable, to remind us that the job of changing hearts and minds is still difficult, necessary, and *ours* to carry on.

Turning onto Calhoun Street, we could almost taste the jubilation that should have been. Normally, the street would have been bustling with horse-drawn carriages loaded with tourists and sidewalks over-whelmed by curious visitors as native Charlestonians buzzed about com-pleting the tasks of their day. But not this Friday. From several blocks away in every direction, hundreds—perhaps thousands—of mourners and sympathizers descended upon Mother Emanuel. Some came in large groups, others in twos, holding hands. Fathers accompanied their toddlers, who held bouquets of flowers larger than their tiny torsos, a dreadful first lesson in sympathy and grief. Some mourners brought single long-stemmed roses while others offered balloons and stuffed animals to memorialize the slain. The sight of perfect strangers weep-ing and consoling each other was moving and remains unforgettable. Drawing closer to the sanctuary, the crowd swelled. So did the silence. If not for the surrounding news trucks, media personalities, and the law enforcement officers managing the traffic, we may not have heard a sound at all at the steps of the church. It seemed that all were represented at Mother Emanuel's feet—black and white, young and old, gay and straight, native and foreign. No race, ethnicity, nationality, or religion was absent from the outpouring of sorrow and haunting solemnity in the dusk's unbearable heat, about which not a single soul complained. This mosaic gathered in mournful accord represented the millions still reeling from the attack.

I returned home to Grovetown, Georgia, a well of uselessness. I had mourned. I had paid my respects. I'd hung my head, chin tucked into chest, in the shadow of the tarnished temple. But it had meant nothing. It had only been a moment squeezed in between shopping, beach comb-ing, eating, drinking, and other thoughtless forms of merrymaking. I was almost frightened at the way I'd been able to compartmentalize the joy and the pain. This tidy separation of grief from elation had become a uniquely American response, and I had mastered it. Days later, I watched President Obama heave "Amazing Grace" from his weariness when words mattered little. He was as useless as me and my tears; as the endless calls for prayers and support on Facebook; as the relentless back-and-forth between liberals and conservatives and the vigils calling for unity; as the twenty-four-hour news coverage with the word MASSACRE screaming in all caps; as every dime raised on GoFundMe to pay for funeral expenses. Utterly useless.

Our responses had been the obligatory, robotic actions of a culture numbed to the black untenable truth at the core of its consciousness: This will happen again, because we are content to take no action to prevent it from happening. Americans going about their daily tasks, engaged in labor or pleasure—attending Sunday-morning church service, going to school, riding their bikes, shopping for groceries, taking in a movie at the cinema, enjoying a concert—will die. Sometimes in fours and fives. Sometimes in tens and twenties. It was just a matter of time.

Charleston, however, held a second significance aside from our national penchant for violence. The Charleston shooting forced many Americans to accept an uncomfortable reality: Racism is alive and well in these United States. It is not a figment of black citizens' imaginations. Racism is a real living, breathing monster that resides in the hearts and minds of some of our neighbors. It didn't disappear with Dr. Martin Luther King Jr. or with President Barack Obama. Racism exists among us. This was a scary thought for a great number of Americans who would've otherwise just wished racism away. And if we understood and accepted that the Charleston shooting had been an act fueled by racism (which it had been), we also had to understand and accept that it had been an act of terrorism. This unsettled some Americans who had come to believe that terror had a singular face—typically male and almost always Muslim or Middle Eastern. These Americans had forgotten that the Ku Klux Klan was among the earliest domestic terror groups formed in the US. Violence upon black churches and black bodies wasn't new. The history of the Deep South was replete with chronicles of lynchings, cross burnings, and murder. Had a young white man shot and killed a group of praying black folks in 1815 or 1915, the incident would have just blended into the backdrop of Southern culture alongside idyllic plantations boasting columned porches and acres of cotton fields.

Three weeks after the murders, Confederate flags started coming down. Some people called it healing. Some people called it progress. I was neither hopeful nor pleased in the slightest by the acts. Symbols do matter; but, in the end, symbols are just symbols—hollow representations of ideas and actions that require courage to change. Perhaps I might have been stirred by the decision to move the Confederate flag from the South Carolina State House grounds to a museum if the price hadn't been so gruesomely high. Nine black people had to be slaughtered for lawmakers to even begin to consider removing the divisive emblem of white supremacy. Perhaps I might not have viewed the removal as political gamesmanship if North Charleston native Walter Scott had been arrested with the same genteel care as the assailant of the Emanuel parishioners. Just two months prior to the massacre, unarmed Walter Scott was shot and killed by a North Charleston police officer. His offenses? A traffic violation and unpaid child support. But the killer of the Charleston Nine was armed and dangerous yet arrested without incident. Erasing the Stars and Bars did nothing to cure the institutional, often invisible, hounding racism that plagues South Carolina and every other state in the union. Perhaps nothing ever will, and that is the central paradox that defines America. How does one come to love a homeland that treats some citizens with seemingly unconditional love and others with disdain?

And yet . . .

The following year, I still longed for the Low Country—to taste the salt at Hilton Head Island, to sip peach moonshine from mason jars at the bistro on Market Street in Charleston, to stumble into unexpected and pleasant conversations with buoyant strangers who turn one-syllable words into two syllables like a song, to watch the Gullah descendants of slaves weave baskets under the cover of tall palmettos, to haggle with dreadlocked parfumiers in the open-air market. Despite the bloodshed and tyranny, I still find something tender about Charleston and all parts of the Deep South. And I think that I've spent the better part of almost four decades now trying to grasp what that tender something is. Sometimes, when I close my eyes and become silent and still, I think I can hear it in my granny's stories, taste it in my great-grandma's sweet tea, imagine it in the pages of Jean Toomer's *Cane*, touch it in the red-clay mud pies of my youth. But exactly what "it" is continually escapes me.

I've not had the opportunity to return to Charleston since the summer of 2015. But when I do, I'll stand in the shadow of Mother Emanuel and remember the pain and the silence. Then I'll look up above her steeple into the endless face of a Carolina sky, remember the resilience and humanity that rose from tragedy, and be filled once again.

Kristie Robin Johnson

On Football, Freedom, and Fear

I love football because my mother loved it. My mother loved football because it was the only thing that my father loved more than her. And I suppose my father loved football because the life of a black man born in 1940 in Augusta, Georgia, was, more often than not, a constant cataloguing of limitations and invisible boundaries that he could forget once he stepped onto the field. In a world where every morning meant asking himself *What will my black skin cost me today?* it had to have been a welcomed relief for a few hours each week during the autumn months to be able to reply *Not one single thing.* My father became a high school football star and played at the college level before suffering a career-ending knee injury that quashed any hopes of life as a professional football player. He died when I was just four years old, leaving behind three children (each with their own complicated, grieving mother) and an obsession with a sport as brutal as it is magnetic.

So, when my wide-eyed six-year-old, my younger child, announced after his first game (which was a loss), "I wanna play football for the rest of my life!" I was thrilled. My fear came later, though not swiftly enough to deter me from getting consumed by the joy in his voice. I thought about my dead father. I thought about my own deferred dreams and subsequent regrets. But more than anything, I thought about my older child who has developmental disabilities. I thought about how the first decade of his life had been weighed down by low expectations and a mile-long list of the things that he couldn't do. I looked at my baby boy's toothless grin and somewhere behind his smile I saw a rekindled relationship with a ghost and redemption for his brother's stolen childhood.

Three years after that first momentous game, I was still tightening pads, still adjusting chin straps, still replacing mouth guards chewed beyond recognition, still lacing up cleats, and still pretending not to worry. I was in the game; but in many ways, I was not. I tried very hard to disassociate myself from the stereotypical football moms and dads: the fathers who had peaked in high school and were living vicariously through their eight-year-old sons; the doting mothers who hid their fears under convenient facts like *More kids get hurt in car accidents than football games*; the parents secretly (or not so secretly) betting on their nine-year-old's throwing arm to one day lift them from the working class to instant wealth; the prevailing "America, fuck yeah!" attitude; the oversized Tundras and F-150s; the bastardized gore and glory of it all. I showed up to practice with books in hand and donned the occasional Black Panther T-shirt to pretend to be different, separate from the pack. I spent half my time at practices with my head buried in the progressive ideas of other writers, wondering if I could call myself a writer yet, and penning my own poems and prose. I tried to spend the other half paying attention to the team. It was the least I could do after signing my kid up to literally risk his neck for some inexplicable and convoluted set of social rules and emotions.

Sister Outsider just happened to arrive in my mailbox on the first day of practice for the 2016 season. The collection of essays and speeches penned by the brilliant and outspoken black lesbian feminist poet Audre Lorde had been on my to-read list for months. I ripped open the packaging with the pent-up excitement of a four-year-old on Christmas Day. The glossy leaf-green cover seemed to glow with the promise of wisdom and truth within the crisp, stark-white pages. But there was no time to indulge. With less than an hour between retrieving the book from the mail and the start of practice, I tossed it into my son's gym bag and rushed off to the field, another season under way.

The first few days of practice could best be described as a cross between military basic training and a summer day trip to Chuck E. Cheese. Dozens of young boys flooded the practice field, separated into regiments by age and weight. To my right were young teens doing sprints. To my left were eight- and nine-year-olds managing cumbersome duck walks, crouched inches from the ground with hands folded behind their heads. In the far corner of the field, a group of boys as young as five were eking out formless push-ups. Women in yoga pants, running shorts, and brightly colored sneakers darted on and off the field with water bottles for the winded and thirsty troops, while men with whistles hanging around their necks and clipboards in their hands barked commands at the children. Even with the sun bearing down on their tender skin and their coaches sometimes turning into drill sergeants, laughter routinely sprung from the swarm of boys. An unexpected bliss seemed to conquer any feelings of fatigue or exhaustion.

Once I delivered my son to his team and coach, I settled into my chair with my coveted text. I scanned the table of contents until I found the most intriguing title, "Man Child: A Black Lesbian Feminist's Response." It felt like an appropriate juxtaposition for a backdrop dripping testosterone and machismo. While I didn't identify as lesbian and probably could only be called a pseudofeminist at best, being a single black mother of two sons drew me into the essay. Despite blaring whistles and the constant thud of cleats galloping back and forth, I slipped into a near-meditative state fixed on Lorde's words.

Her voice echoed in my head as I underlined passages with urgency. "I give the most strength to my children by being willing to look within myself, and by being honest with them about what I find there, without expecting a response beyond their years. In this way they begin to learn to look beyond their own fears." I asked myself, Had I been honest with my son? Did he fully understand that the reasons I let him play were to remember my daddy, to find some cosmic sense of justice for his brother, and to quell my fear that he might turn out like me, waiting until he's thirty-five to summon enough courage to pursue his true passion? Could he even comprehend such a long, drawn-out explanation? Did he know how severely out of place I felt there on the sidelines with the other, clearly more enthusiastic, parents? Was that something I should even discuss with a nine-year-old? Audre posed too many questions. Splats of water began to dot the pages. I lifted my head to see black clouds in the distance and folks rushing in every direction like ants fleeing a disturbed mound. I'd have to postpone questioning my parenting skills until later.

The ride home was short, wet, and pensive. I kept glancing over at my son, Patrick, in the passenger seat, staring at the gray skies and swirling clouds that had so cruelly conspired to ruin his practice. It was hard to guess what he was thinking. I supposed he was most likely pondering whether he'd land a running-back position this year or whether I'd stop by McDonald's on the way home. But sometimes Patrick would get a certain look in his eyes, an impenetrable gaze full of pre-pubescent longing that couldn't be deciphered. It was the unsung secret that boys always keep from their mothers. With Lorde lingering on my mind, I broke the silence.

"Pat, you know that you can stop playing whenever you get ready? Right?"

"Huh?"

"Football. You can stop playing whenever you're ready."

"I don't wanna stop playing."

"I know. I just wanted you to know that you can stop when you're ready. Just say the word."

"Mom, what are you talking about?"

"Never mind."

I was pretty sure that pitiful and forced conversation didn't make him any braver and only succeeded in revealing my unsureness about the whole football thing.

I routinely shied away from the notorious concussion discussion that always arose with liberal acquaintances and elderly women whenever I shared that my son played football. I had no explanation that embraced any semblance of logic. At all. I felt embarrassed because I knew that their concerns were girded with science and truth.

I felt equally embarrassed every time Patrick and I were in a grocery store or Walmart after a game and some broad-grinned, middle-aged, well-meaning white man in a baseball cap looked down (almost lov-ingly) at my child, still in his pads and cleats, and asked, *Who do you play for, big guy?* or *Did you guys win?*, silently welcoming him in to an ancient, artificial notion of manhood. I resisted the urge to blurt out, "He's an honor roll student!" to erase any bias they may have had (never mind the fact I had completely prejudged them). Patrick always answered politely, just as I'd taught him. I always walked away from those moments wondering if my son would have been a menace in the eyes of those men if he had been wearing a hoodie and sporting dreadlocks or cornrows. Did his uniform make him acceptable? Was it a sign to good ol' boys meaning *He's one of us*? It's odd. The game that seemed to liberate my father from a racist reality was the same game that seemed to trap my son in a tradition and stereotype that should have passed away decades before he was born.

Too perplexed to sleep that night, I picked up "Man Child" from where I'd left off. I read about Lorde's son, Jonathan, and his striving to define manhood for himself in a time far less progressive and forward-thinking than our own. I thought I'd finish the essay ready to decry football as the dangerous, barbaric, patriarchal sport that it is and ban my child from playing whether he liked it or not. But that's not what I felt at all. "Man Child" reminded me that my children were not *mine*. They, Patrick and Bobby, ultimately belong to only themselves and to no one else. My job, as the vessel responsible for bringing them into this world, was to find a way to prepare them for what lies ahead and to do this with as much honesty and love as possible.

I put the book down and remembered who I was. I was the woman who was unwilling to stay in a loveless marriage one second longer than she needed to, no matter how unclear the path ahead seemed. I was the woman who marched into her boss's office, resignation letter in hand, with no other job secured, ready to see a lifelong dream through to its very end. I was the woman who put her autistic twelve-year-old on a plane flying from Atlanta to Denver by himself. I was *that* chick. I realized in that moment that the most important thing I could do for my babies was to try to teach them to live free for themselves through my own imperfect example.

Sometime between 9/11 and my mother's untimely passing in 2006, I discovered that there was no such thing as safe. Safety is an idea created in the minds of modern human beings to provide us with a false sense of immunity from the inevitability of danger and death. When my mother died in her sleep at the too-soon age of fifty-five, I made a conscious decision to rethink the way I allowed fear to function in my life. From that point forward, whenever I was presented with a critical choice, instead of letting my brain fill to capacity with all the terrible possibilities of moving in the direction of the unknown, I chose to worry about what might happen if I didn't. I learned to fear regret instead of failure. I was five months pregnant with Patrick when my mother died, and I like to think that he inherited my renewed outlook on life.

I don't know a single human being who understands the value of play the way that Patrick does. From the second he took his first breath, it appeared that he adored movement, frolic, laughter. He seemed overcome by the desire to dance even before he could walk. Football is just one of the many ways he has found to express joy through action and play in his brief nine years. He has taken karate lessons and run track as well, but nothing has lit up his world the way football does. To tear him away from his passion would be the same as someone telling me that I'd never be able to write again.

But I still had the responsibility of putting football into context for him. After all, it is just a game. It was my job to remind Patrick that what he does on the field doesn't define him; to remind him that the purpose of pain is to signal the need for rest, water, cleansing gulps of air; to allow him to express himself even when that expression is through tears and to not tear him down for doing so; to teach him that true power is not a matter of physical might, but one of mental fortitude, that his ability to think critically and speak freely for himself is more precious than any record set on a forty-yard dash, or any number of tackles made or touchdowns scored.

All season long, I struggled with the contradiction, the internal conflict that pitted me against myself. As much as I wanted to be perceived as intelligent, rational, and professorial, I also just wanted my kid to be happy. The current football culture in this nation leaves much to be desired with its obvious violence, promotion of toxic masculinity, and obsession with material wealth above all else. It isn't only football culture that's damaging, though; it's American culture as a whole. Football is just symptomatic of our greater cultural ailment. Major cultural change always begins from within. I decided that as long as Patrick wanted to play football and maintained strong grades, he would play football. There are those who argue that the lessons of sportsmanship, teamwork, discipline, and physical fitness render football a sport that can be beneficial to many kids. This is not untrue, but very few consider how individuals can be beneficial to the sport. It occurred to me that if I could hearken to Lorde's call to raise my son with honesty and without fear, he could very well grow into a man who is good for the game of football—an independent-thinking athlete who is unafraid of self-expression, who values knowledge over physical prowess, who isn't a slave to the trappings of success.

I eventually finished most of Lorde's essays right out there on the field during Patrick's practices. I lifted my head from my book from time to time and even began to strike up conversations with other moms—first, about the weather and, later, about other nuisances. I soon learned that we were more alike than unalike. None of us wanted our sons to be violent brutes. All of us wanted our children to be happy. I could still be a thinker, a writer, a peace-loving panther, and a proud football mom. I had nothing to be ashamed of. This was my version of breathing free.

Kristie Robin Johnson

Shame the Devil

I was taught to be strong. I was taught to be respectful. I was taught to follow the rules. I was taught to look people in the eye and to never ask a man for anything. I was taught to never cry in front of others (shows weakness). I was taught what it meant to be ladylike—crossed legs, closed mouth, muted lipstick, brimming with virtue, waiting for a husband, sexless. I was taught that a strong black woman is a warrior, never a victim.

In the summer of 1998, I was eighteen years old and living in Atlanta, Georgia—a pulsing city, two hours away from home, thick with opportunity and danger and an urban heat that rose from the asphalt, bounced off the skyscrapers, and slapped you right in the face. Atlanta was a goal, a trophy, a finish line to be crossed for ambitious, young black folks. Atlanta represented a kind of gold-plated elegance that couldn't be found in Augusta. If you really want to impress an Augustan, just tell them that you purchased your expensive purse, sneakers, car, jewelry, or cosmetic surgery in Atlanta and watch envy drip from the pores of their skin. I had moved to the South's premier metropolis in August 1997 to attend Georgia State University (GSU). I lived with my godmother in Riverdale, an Atlanta suburb, and commuted to the city each day to go to class and to work at Parisian, a department store in Phipps Plaza. By May 1998, I had a boyfriend who worked at Enterprise Rent-A-Car in Midtown Atlanta and lived in Stone Mountain. I had a hair stylist in Lithonia. I had a best friend who worked at the airport and another close friend who lived in the Allen Temple projects in the Adamsville neighborhood of Atlanta. I was a regular at Dugan's restaurant on east Ponce de Leon. I took the MARTA at Indian Creek to Falcons football games. I parked at Turner

Field and caught the shuttle to GSU when the Braves were on the road. I was something that neither my mother nor my grandmother had ever been—a city girl.

One night as I was leaving work, an acquaintance I had met at a get-together at my godmother's house asked for a ride home. I knew him well enough. He was an older dude with a sketchy past, but he was friendly, with fat, round eyes and a contagious laugh. He flirted with me on occasion, but I never took him seriously. He was a jokester, and everyone liked him. He'd even worked on my car when I didn't have enough money to put it in the shop. I didn't think twice about giving him the ride.

When we pulled up at his nondescript, ranch-style home in southwest Atlanta, he asked me to come inside for a drink. I waffled. Then he insisted. It was dark, but not yet late, not even 10:00 p.m., and, after all, I was a city girl. It seemed perfectly reasonable that a chic and worldly city girl like me would have a drink with a friend after work, share a few laughs, then head home.

Upon entrance, the interior was unimpressive—sparse furniture, shag carpeting—but not unusual for a man living alone. I took a seat on the faux leather couch and waited until he returned from the kitchen, all smiles, with two cans of Budweiser in his hands. I cracked open my can and took short sips as I listened to him talk about his new job and trying to get back on his feet. His conversation was animated by his trademark humor and exaggerated gulps of beer. For a moment, I thought he was priming me to ask for money. But he didn't. He finished his beer before I even drank half of mine. Then he put his can down and leaned in to kiss me. I recoiled. "I've got a boyfriend," I said, fully believing that was more than enough of an explanation for not wanting to kiss this guy.

He put his hands on my waist and pulled me toward him. "C'mon. What's that got to do with anything?" His words were muffled because his mouth was buried in my neck at this point. I put my hands on his forearms to push him away and that's when I felt the entire weight of his body force me backwards onto the couch.

He tried to kiss me on the mouth again. I turned away. "Please stop!" He pretended not to hear me. He pushed up my skirt, yanked my panties to the side, and forced himself inside of me. I closed my eyes tight and prayed to somehow sink into the cheap sofa and disappear. His mouth was sloppy and wet and frantic. The smell of cigarettes, beer, and sweat swirled

114

in my nostrils. His hands were heavy and calloused, his grip unforgiving. The sound of his pot belly slapping into mine was as earsplitting as it was revolting. I lay underneath him stunned, baffled at the ease with which he discarded my "nos" and "stops." Had I said anything to entice him? Had I smiled too much? Had I dressed too provocatively?

He released this awful moan, full of satisfaction and relief, and collapsed on top of me, gasping for air, his damp body smothering mine. I slid from underneath him, twisted my skirt back into place, grabbed my keys, and bolted for the door. He yelled something behind me, but I have no idea what he said. I just needed to get to my car and get out.

I couldn't go home to my godmother's house. I couldn't go to my boyfriend's apartment. I couldn't *go* anywhere. I just drove. I circled I-285 until daybreak. When the sun pierces the golden dome of the Georgia State Capitol, it can be spectacular, even breathtaking, but that morning I didn't notice it, and I never would again. Suddenly, this city that had painted me sophisticated, trendy, and smart felt terrifying and soulless. It had conquered me, I hadn't conquered it.

By the time I finally returned to my godmother's house, she was waiting at the door with a barrage of questions: "Where have you been! I was worried sick! Why didn't you answer your phone? What's gotten into you! Have you lost your ever-loving mind?" I lied and said I'd gone out with coworkers, had too much to drink, and stayed at one of their houses until I sobered up. I apologized and then plodded up the stairs and hopped in the shower.

I was taught to remain steely and stoic at all times and never to show too much skin. I was taught to never be a tease or lead guys on. I was taught to never dance too closely, never thrust my hips into his crotch. I was taught to shun alcohol because girls who drink are "loose." I was taught to be careful of the company I keep, that girls who laugh too loud, live too free, are bad influences. I was taught to remain tight-lipped about the sensation that stirs my center when a man kisses me and I, somehow, like it. I was taught to fight and not trust. I was taught to exist and not live. I was taught all the things that would make me chaste, respectable, and virtually rape proof.

＊

115

I didn't tell anyone—not my mother, not my godmother, not my best friend, not my boyfriend. I didn't call the police. There was no report filed. There was no rape kit. Nothing. Like the overwhelming majority of women who are raped or sexually assaulted in the US, I remained silent. What was there to tell? I'd broken the rules, forgotten my place. I'd mistaken myself for a man—a being who owns their sexual agency, one who can take liberty in visiting friends of the opposite sex after dark and never have to worry about being assaulted. If I'd just remembered to remain pristine and flawless and faultless behind the glass of patriarchy, morality, and double standards, then I wouldn't have been raped.

At the time, I placed the blame on myself. So, I never reported the attack. I just stepped out of the shower and carried on. I avoided my assailant on his rare visits to my godmother's house. If he was going to be at a cookout or a Sunday dinner, I made sure I was scheduled to work or went to a friend's house. By the time I moved back to Augusta in 1999, I had taken his name, face, and all memories of that night and filed them under the NEVER EVER OPEN EVER tab in my brain. It would take sixteen years, two children, one failed marriage, hundreds of hours of self-reflection, and one highly publicized celebrity sexual assault scandal before I could revisit that scar and break an unbreakable silence.

By the time the Bill Cosby scandal broke in 2014, I had become an obnoxiously typical American—a midlevel employee with two kids, a house in suburban hell, and a marriage that had just dissolved after seven years of faked happiness. I hadn't achieved the success of Cliff and Clair Huxtable, but I had tried. *The Cosby Show* had been the representation of what the pinnacle of an overachieving black upper middle class could look like in America. The show was so seductive because it not only depicted African Americans as equal citizens worthy of the stability and wealth they had worked to create but was also the brainchild of a black American icon. Cosby cast a long and unyielding shadow on the concepts of black respectability and racial pride. So, when the initial reports of rape allegations against Cosby began to surface, many people of all races balked at the idea that this hero could be capable of such heinous acts.

At the time, I was an opinion columnist for the local black newspaper, and everyone wanted to know what I thought. As the accusers began to pile one on top of the other, I tried to avoid conversations about Cosby. I dodged coworkers in the break room, abruptly changed the subject when talking with friends. No one knew me to be a rape survivor, but everyone pegged me as militant. They expected me to rail against the mostly white accusers and their supposedly vicious lies. They expected me to defend Dr. Cosby as a respected bastion of African American leadership. They would've preferred me to label the whole situation a smear campaign maliciously aimed at muddying Bill Cosby's good name. They wanted me to join in the chorus bellowing, *They're after his money*, and *Why did they wait so long to come forward?* I avoided the conversations because I knew what it was like to hoard pain in a box of silence and swallow the key. I knew, based on the number of women who came forward, that he'd probably done it. I knew that if I acknowledged their bravery, I, too, would have to unearth my own uncomfortable truth.

What was more, confronting the Cosby situation head-on would require me to nearly split my being in half. I would be forced to choose whether my first loyalty was to being black or to being female. African American women often find themselves at this awkward crossroads when prominent black men are accused of sexual assault or domestic violence. For centuries, black male sexuality had been (and sometimes still is) a scapegoat for race-based violence and murder. Emmett Till was kidnapped and murdered because he was accused of flirting with a white woman. Countless lynchings of black men were justified by the false rape accusations of white women. An entire Florida town was reduced to ashes in 1923 because a white woman falsely accused a black man of assaulting her. So, today, when African American men are accused, the knee-jerk reaction of the average black woman is to say, *He didn't do it; she's lying*, because black men have a visible history of being framed for sex crimes. To be black and not support Bill Cosby unequivocally was a racial cardinal sin.

I knew better. I had already been maligned years earlier when I suggested that consumers boycott R. Kelly concerts after videos surfaced of him having lewd sex with a fourteen-year-old girl. Grown women routinely defended this man, suggesting that the teenager was "fast" and had tempted the R & B star intentionally. And when pictures of Rihanna's bruised, swollen face were released in 2009 after Chris Brown beat her, I got into shouting matches with other black women trying to convince them there was no provocation that could have justified his brutality.

I was not mentally prepared to examine my real feelings about Cosby and his accusers. Engaging in the debate would have forced me to concede that I had been raped by a funny, well-liked black man, yet had told no one and had done nothing about it. I didn't want to be labeled a coward, which was how I felt, or a whore, as R. Kelly's victim was called, or an antagonist who deserved what she got, similar to how Rihanna was described.

The truth was that it took years for me to realize and admit that I had been raped. An even harder truth was accepting the possibility that my rapist never understood what he had done to me as wrong, much less criminal. We had both been raised in a world where boys would be boys and girls were expected to be virginal, pure, asexual beings. It occurred to me that, perhaps, my attack did not begin on that horrible May night in 1998. Maybe it began the second I was born with a double-X chromosomal profile in a society where we allow our sons to experience the full range of human emotion—anger, sadness, fear, hope, love, lust—but our daughters must grow up loving without lusting, never experiencing a physical yearning or sexual desire. It occurred to me that the expectation of purity may well have been the very beginning of the victimization of countless women and girls. The right to be both sex-seeking and sex-taking remained exclusively in the domain of manhood.

The women who raised me had been made of steel, welded together by tenacity and grace. But in whispers and private conversations they'd told me tales of abortions, extramarital affairs, domestic violence—secrets that physically hurt to say aloud. My grandmother and I shucked fresh corn while she told me about the moment she knew she'd fallen in love with a married man. I had been painting my mother's fingernails when she disclosed that she'd terminated a pregnancy at seventeen years old. An older, trusted friend once shared with me that she'd grown so tired of her husband's physical abuse, she'd gotten in the habit of keeping a pot of boiling water on her stove, prepared to scald him before he could punch her; we'd been cooking pasta for dinner when she shared the memory. No one ever confessed to having been raped. It seemed like the one thing that remained too tragic to speak of, the leper of all things hidden. So, when it did happen to me, I struggled to find ways to make it seem as though it hadn't happened at all.

Staying mum didn't quiet the cacophony between my ears, though, so I began the odious task of convincing myself that I hadn't truly been raped. I told myself that since he didn't don a mask and gloves or hold me at knifepoint, at most the whole episode had just been an unfortunate misunderstanding. When feeding myself that fable didn't stop the bad dreams or numb the shame, I drank until all the memories dissipated into a blur. I spent my last year in Atlanta as a veritable weekend drunk. I dropped out of school but kept my job. Most of my days off were spent binge drinking until I blacked out.

Unorthodox and destructive as it had been, my system had worked. Years passed, and I forgot the incident. It wasn't until I'd been married five years that I was even reminded of the attack. My husband and I were parked on the sofa, zombified by a daylong thunderstorm and a *Law & Order: SVU* marathon. One episode depicted a classic he said/she said case involving a male professor and his female student. Unlike most episodes, this particular story didn't lead viewers to a definite conclusion. The writers allowed the resolution to remain hazy, mimicking the reality for thousands of victims of sexual assault. My husband rose to his feet at end of the show. "Eh, she's lying," he growled.

"How would you know?" I retorted, annoyed by his attitude.

"I mean you can tell when a girl really means 'No.'"

"What!"

"Yeah. Say you're with a girl and y'all are kissing and you start to unzip her . . ."

"Are you fucking kidding me?" I shouted and stomped up the stairs, so mad that my ears felt like they were on fire. I slammed the bedroom door behind me, and everything came rushing back—the sticky leather, his clammy skin against mine, the gravel in his voice, his giant bloodshot eyes. The recollection startled me, left me breathless. Later that night, my husband said I'd been too sensitive and told me that's just how things were in his day. But even in that moment, I wasn't brave enough to tell my own spouse what had happened to me. I still couldn't find the words to admit the truth.

*

119

I was taught to fry my husband's chicken in a heavy, cast-iron skillet. I was taught to use light starch when ironing the collars on his work shirt and to fix his plate each night at dinner. I was taught to make our marriage bed with tight hospital corners. I was taught to wash our baby's clothes in Dreft. I was taught to dust on Saturdays and mop on Mondays.

After about two months of ducking Cosby questions, I walked into my coworker's office, pulled the door behind me, sat down slowly in the seat across from her, raised my eyes to her face, and took a deep breath.

"Melvin. His name was Melvin."

I fought back tears as I released the name of my rapist into the universe, the name that had lived in the recesses of my subconscious for sixteen years. I wasn't telling the world, but I was finally telling somebody. My coworker listened to me and cried with me. We were two brown women breaking all the rules—being vulnerable, showing feelings, shedding the armor that was supposed to make us invincible. It was in this moment that I realized it wasn't our statuesque stoicism or our stubborn reluctance to emote that rendered us unbreakable. It was, indeed, these instances of intimacy and exposure, when we dared to remove our masks and beheld each other and chose to love rather than judge each other, that fortified us. I was stronger for facing my past and speaking the truth.

I've never been quite sure what force led me into her office that morning. It could've been the daily inundation of Cosby coverage on the television, in the newspapers, on the blogs and social media. It could've been a subconscious need to release the weight of the secret. It could've been the fact that I had seven-year-old and fourteen-year-old sons who were watching the scandal unfold and I desperately desired for them to not turn out like their dad—believing a woman's word to be disposable, her body not always her own. I couldn't allow them to grow up thinking themselves beasts incapable of self-control and, therefore, absolved of all responsibility for their own sexual proclivities. They needed to know that no number of honorary degrees, Grammy Awards, or good deeds could erase the perpetual taint of violating a woman (or a man, for that matter). They needed to understand that they could not hurt others without forever damaging themselves.

Releasing myself from my own shame would be the first step in offering them that education.

Fast-forward to November 2017. Harvey Weinstein, Tavis Smiley, Al Franken, Kevin Spacey, Russell Simmons, Charlie Rose, Roy Moore, Matt Lauer—all now disgraced household names connected to a movement that asks women to step out of the centuries-long shadow, be seen and heard, and create courage out of what was once shame.

The Sunday before Thanksgiving, the movement became literal dinner table conversation in my home. I wondered aloud how powerful men must now be living day to day, retreading their steps, reexamining their lives, and praying that their past bad actions didn't resurface to destroy them. Unexpectedly, my ex-husband agreed with me and suggested that the reckoning had been long overdue.

"Well, you know, Hollywood has always had a problem. You know, with the casting couch and all that type of stuff."

"Ken," I interrupted. "Do you think this is appropriate to talk about in front of the kids?"

Then our youngest son said, "I know what the casting couch is," his eyes as wide and bright as the day he was born.

"Tell me what you know about the casting couch. Where did you learn about it?" I asked feigning calm, not wanting to reveal my inner horror. I imagined my eleven-year-old perusing Pornhub videos on his phone.

At first, he only offered a nervous grin. I returned a raised eyebrow of insistence, and his father shot a glare in his direction as well. "It's when people have sex to get on TV. I saw it on *Law & Order: SVU*."

"Okay," I replied, relieved. "Do you understand why that's wrong?"

"Yeah." He paused for a moment. "There's no dignity."

I nodded in approval. I wanted to lecture him about abuse, coercion, and patriarchal power structures. But he was only eleven, and his dinner was getting cold. I took pride in the fact that he was comfortable enough to say the word "sex" at the dinner table. I was never liberated enough to have that type of conversation with my mother at his age. And my grandmother would've slapped me across my mouth for such boldness. Thankfully, times have changed and are still changing. A watershed moment, indeed.

Always in April

Then the Lord God said to the woman, "What is this you have done?" The woman said, "The serpent deceived me, and I ate."
—Genesis 3:13 (New International Version)

My grandmother was a snake slayer and she probably came from a long line of snake slayers. Snake sightings were a common occurrence for her, having been raised in the thick, oppressive steam of a Lincolnton, Georgia, farmstead. Her younger brothers learned to befriend the creatures, handled them gently, and used them to pull pranks on less brave Lincolntonians. The most common species she reported encountering were small garter snakes and the occasional water moccasin. I don't know if it was out of simple necessity, an attempt to fit in with the boys, or the same awful dread that chokes me every time I see one, but somehow, she cultivated a talent and a reputation for killing snakes. Her preferred method was using the sharp edge of a garden hoe to chop off the heads of serpents. Like terrorists cloaked in flowing black raiments, headless infidels slept at her feet.

*

In general, snakes tend to get a bad rap. This can be connected to the pervasiveness of Christianity in modern culture. The Bible depicts the serpent as a symbol of evil and the embodiment of Satan himself in the book of Revelation. Saint Patrick is said to have expelled all snakes from Ireland as he converted the country to Christianity in the fifth century.

Incidentally, my youngest son's name is Patrick, and he has penchant for killing lizards that he finds in our backyard.

*

I am afraid of snakes. It's one of the only fears that I claim in public and it is rooted in nothing more than illogical hysteria. Though I've never been harmed by a snake, just a picture of the reptile fills me with an overwhelming anxiety. My chest tightens. My heartbeat accelerates. The insides of my palms begin to moisten and every cell in my body labors in unison to look away. I have no idea when or where this fear began. I often feel that I arrived with this fear. It's as much a part of me as my brown eyes, black hair, and wide nose. When I try to find the true origin of this phobia, I'm quickly reminded of the infectious folklore of the snake—the evil tempter, the cursed charlatan, the cause for all human iniquity.

*

According to no less than twenty-one internet self-help gurus, one overpaid clinical psychologist, two marriage counselors, and my invincible grandmother, the best way to conquer your fear is to embrace it. No one ever suggested running in the opposite direction.

*

I once loved a snake. For the sake of storytelling, let's call him Mike. He reminds me of the first snake I ever learned about in Sunday school. He was biblical and quiet in his coming, and quite convincing, too. The temptation was invisible, intoxicating, complete.

*

Snakes use their sense of smell to track down prey. They use their infamous forked tongues to transmit particles from the air to their vomeronasal organ located in the back of their mouth. Their tongues remain virtually in constant motion as they sample and analyze the chemicals in their environment. Some species have infrared-sensitive receptors that allow them to "see" the warmth of the blood of mammals. Even in complete darkness, they can detect the radiated heat pouring off their warm-blooded targets long before those animals realize that they are about to strike.

*

Mike must have smelled the odor of congealed loneliness through the computer screen, tasted it over the phone.

He remembered me from high school—our hands touching in a darkened movie theater, my hand finding the growing bulge below his belt. He remembered a nervousness most men don't admit to feeling. He remembered sweat from his forehead causing his glasses to slide down the bridge of his nose. He remembered dropping me off at my grandmother's house that evening, heart still pounding, trying to think awful thoughts to suppress his erection. He remembered rushing home to the coldest shower ever.

I remembered feeling powerful, like a sorcerer or an all-knowing temptress. I remembered giggling when I told my best girlfriend about the date. I remembered finding his inexperience cute and oddly magnetic. I remembered not being able to wait to see him again.

Twenty years later, somehow I'm the unsuspecting novice—the freshly divorced, sexless, isolated single mother—ripe for the plucking. And he's the one laughing (I suppose). He's married but says he's unhappy. He says that he just wants to catch up over drinks, but his hands are under my shirt, tugging at my jeans. He says that I've always understood him, that she doesn't. He sends text messages at three in the morning then disappears, sometimes for weeks at a time. He apologizes like a real boyfriend but doesn't call on my birthday, Christmas, or Valentine's Day.

*

Most people understand snake charming to be an ancient tradition originating in India. The charmer carries a basket that contains a snake that he seemingly charms by playing melodies from a flutelike instrument to which the animal responds. Snakes lack external ears. They respond to the movement of the flute, not the sound. Snake charming as a practice was officially banned in India in 1991 by an expansion of the Wildlife Protection Act of 1972 on the grounds of animal cruelty. Snake charming has decreased significantly in popularity in India because of competition from modern forms of entertainment. YouTube strikes again.

*

When I was fourteen, I stepped out of the bathroom of my grandmother's house, where we were living, and noticed something odd in the hallway near my bedroom door. Wedged between the edge where the carpet met the wall was a slim shadow. At first glance, it could've been a cord or a shoestring, but an eerie suspicion told me it could have been something else, something far more menacing. Perhaps a bit of my grandmother's blood kicked in or maybe I really believed it was just a shadow when I slowly stretched my big toe as far from the rest of my body as I could and barely, barely touched the mystery just outside my bedroom. It moved, and my heart plummeted to the very bottom of my gut. I retracted my foot, but I didn't run or even scream. It was in this exact moment that I realized all fears are not created equal. Some fears syphon the air out of your lungs, leaving you hollow, lifeless, immobilized. Somehow, I made my way down the hall and into the kitchen. "There's a snake in the house," I announced to my mother without any real inflection, still suspended in a zombielike state. My mother did what I couldn't—she bolted. She ran out of the house and kept running until she reached the fence at the furthest end of the backyard. I followed her lead.

The first and most obvious inclination was to call my grandmother, the snake slayer. But she couldn't come to our rescue right away. She was caring for her ailing mother and couldn't leave until her sister came to relieve her caregiving duties. Neither my mother nor I was willing to return inside until we knew the monster was gone. So, we did what civil people are expected to do when an unwanted intruder has invaded their home—we called 911. We lived in the type of neighborhood where the arrival of cop cars signified a free, front-row ticket to whatever calamity has brought them there. It was really a sort of impoverished pastime. Within minutes, the cul-de-sac buzzed with nosy onlookers. The first policeman to arrive was, to our astonishment, just as frightened as we were. He tiptoed through the front door an unsteady but obligated sleuth, reminiscent of Shaggy and Scooby-Doo from the popular cartoon. A palpable relief spread across his face and all over his body when the second cop arrived. This man was special, almost magical. He got out of his cruiser with some type of instrument that looked like an untwisted wire hanger. He took one step into our living room and sniffed the air. "Yep, there's a snake in here." I got the sense that he wasn't a slayer like my grandmother. He was a charmer. He asked the first officer to step outside. He and the serpent required privacy. My mother and I, officer number one, and about seven or eight neighbors that had gathered for the show stood in the front yard waiting for the charmer.

After about fifteen minutes, he emerged with a rather small brown snake wrapped around his hand and wrist. His chest puffed with heroic pride. "What are you going to do with it?" chirped one of the younger bystanders.

"I'll probably drive him a few miles down the highway and let him go in the woods."

I couldn't believe it. A snake had survived his venture into a snake slayer's house. My grandmother pulled up shortly after the scene had cleared. We excitedly relayed every horrific detail to her as we tiptoed into the house. Even though my grandmother brought a certain calm with her arrival, sleep was uneasy for both me and my mother that night. The next day, my grandmother spread sulfur around the perimeter of the house and along the fence. She completed the ritual by ordering us out of the house as she burned a small portion, no more than two or three ounces, of the chalky yellow substance, allowing the poisonous vapor to fill the tiny structure. We couldn't return until nightfall. We never saw a snake inside the house again.

*

In the United States, you are most likely to encounter a snake during the warmer months of the year. Like many other creatures, snakes go into a state of winter dormancy during the colder months. It's not actual hibernation because the snakes do not go to sleep for the entire season. They brumate in the winter, remaining awake but inactive.

✳

Every time an actual living snake has crossed my path, it has always been in April. The small garter that slithered its way into my grandmother's house visited in April 1994. The one that paralyzed me on my own patio showed up in April 2015. And the last time I saw one was this past April, crossing a busy highway in Milledgeville, Georgia, arduously pushing his belly across the stinging asphalt.

I am reminded of T. S. Eliot's description from *The Waste Land*: "April is the cruelest month, breeding / Lilacs out of the dead land, mixing / Memory and desire, stirring / Dull roots with spring rain." I am reminded that it was in April when John Wilkes Booth finally got up the nerve and made his way to the theater. I am reminded how April saw James Earl Ray's bullet split the crisp Memphis air and the consciousness of an entire nation. Who knew spring could be so deceitful?

After about six weeks of silence, my phone lit up in the second week of April with a text from Mike. "You good?"

"Thought you forgot about me. I'm good. How are you?"

"Just been busy. Got a lot going on. The boys home?"

"I should've known that you weren't just being nice."

"What's that supposed to mean?"

"You only call when you're in town and horny."

"For the record, I'm actually not in town. I just wanted to talk to you about my situation. But don't worry about it. Sorry I hit you up."

"If you just wanted to talk, why does it matter where my kids are? And, for the record, when have you ever called just to talk? You can't be mad at me."

Always in April.

✳

Like other creatures in the wild, male snakes will often engage in ritual battle with each other for the right to mate with certain females. Once the dominant male has established himself, he mates with the female by using his tail to grip the walls of the female's cloaca. For some lucky snakes this whole process is optional because they have the ability to reproduce asexually through a process called parthenogenesis.

*

The last time that we fucked, he said he loved me. He said that he'd moved out of his home with his wife. He said he'd do anything in the world for me and invited me to accompany him on a business trip. "We need to spend time outside of these four walls." He laid me on my belly and pushed himself inside me—slower, more tender than ever before. He kissed the back of my neck, grazed his teeth across my shoulder blades just before the point of biting. He teased my spine with the tip of his tongue. An electric current ran through me. The sensation caused me to squirm and twist underneath his weight. I dozed off smiling in an absolute stupor, his left arm wrapped around me.

I tried, but I could never stay asleep while Mike was lying next to me. I just lay there counting the breaths between his nodding off and the sun's inevitable appearance. I prayed to somehow stop it, not forever, but for a few more precious hours. I coveted those rare, dark minutes that I lay beside him watching his chest rise and fall, watching his lungs fill with what was left of us and exhale the secrets of a dream. I ran the tips of my fingers over the hills of his chest and shoulders. I imagined they were beautiful dunes of Saharan sand crafted by God himself. *Him*self? I questioned myself for a moment, then swiftly slipped back into the endless desert of his arms.

He awoke vigilant and hurried, as if the night before had been some tumultuous dream—the kind you wish to scrub violently from your memory but can't. He didn't stretch. He didn't greet the sun. He threw on his clothes nearly as fast as he had removed them and headed down the steps.

I followed, desperate to hang on to every second. "You said Tuesday, the seventh. Right?"

He seemed to have already forgotten about the business-trip invitation. "Oh, yeah. Yeah, I'll call you." He leaned in for a kiss. I obliged, a terrible habit of mine—obliging to Mike. A sobering truth poured over me. I'd never hear from him again.

I didn't let my faith in him falter quickly. I waited three or four days before I sent the first text message, to which there was no reply. I waited two more days before I called. No answer. Still, I couldn't allow the truth to set in. I made the same excuses I had always made—he's busy, he's sorting things out, he's complicated.

The seventh came and went. I cried in the shower for three nights straight, too embarrassed to look at myself in the mirror. Consumed by shame for having been so willingly smitten by a married man, I counted the number of times we'd seen each other since the day we reconnected—and by seen, I mean had some type of encounter always marked with minimal foreplay, rough sex, and meaningless conversation, none of which ever lasted more than five or six hours. Seven times. Five late nights, one early morning, and one cloudy Tuesday afternoon, all strung together with dazzling lies in the shape of IMs, text messages, and a few strategically placed phone calls. I'd only laid eyes on him seven times over the course of a year. The humiliation stung worse than any wasp or bee sting or angry fire-ant bite.

*

Human deaths resulting from snakebites are uncommon, if not rare. The bite of a nonvenomous snake is harmless. Their teeth aren't sharp enough to tear flesh or inflict a deep puncture wound. Even bites from venomous snakes aren't likely to be fatal.

In 2015, at least five people died in the United States from fatal snakebites: Russell, Grant, Gilbert, David, and John David. Most of them died from the accidental bite of rattlesnakes. Grant's death was ruled a suicide. He apparently killed himself by allowing his pet monocled cobra to bite him.

*

One must forgive the reptilian brain that doesn't understand the idiom of love.

*

The Psychology 101 of my youth described the human brain as divided into three sections: reptilian, limbic, and neocortex. The reptilian section is the oldest in terms of human evolution and is devoted primarily to basic survival and functions purely upon impulse. It is incapable of consciousness or discernment. The reptilian brain is aggressive, greedy, and sex-seeking. Some popular psychology theories suggest that humans will only reach their highest level of brain functioning or "true manifestation potential" when we learn to bypass the reptilian brain in favor of the limbic and neocortex sections, which are associated with empathy, logic, and awareness.

*

Eventually I stopped waiting for Mike. I deleted his messages and number from my phone and unfriended him on Facebook. I made him an apparition, a memory, something that used to be. The healing was slow but visible. Gradually, I took back everything that I had given away—my beautiful black-girl confidence, my wee morning hours and pitch-black nights, my crooked grin and billowing laugh, my faith in love, my bent but unbroken heart. After a while even the things that reminded me of him became tolerable again, such as the color yellow and sappy love songs and *Seinfeld* reruns and Braves games and vintage bottles of Glenlivet scotch and tiny Southern towns like Estill and Camak.

And one day it occurred to me that I am my grandmother's granddaughter. I, too, am one of a long line of snake slayers.

Three Poems for Pedro

Saturday, June 17, 2017

We were beautiful that night, Farren and I, in our white dresses, black ringlets framing my face and her hair pulled back into a regal bun. The picture we took in front of the step and repeat banner was reminiscent of so many pictures we'd taken over the previous thirty-three years: me on the right and Farren on the left, my head tilted slightly towards her shoulder as if drawn in by a magnet, her (taller) leaning into me like a mother nestling her young—protective and endearing—an uncommon affection between two black women. This was the pose that had defined our friendship. It was the way we captured ourselves in selfies at a Falcons game in 2016, front row at a Mary J. Blige concert in 2015, in my overpriced wedding photos in 2006, dressed in satin and sequins at my grandmother's seventy-fifth birthday celebration in 1999, the night of our debutante ball in 1997.

We were leaving the white party to have drinks when I asked Farren if she minded that I had invited a man to join us whom I'd met the night before at a Latin nightclub. I told her that he was Puerto Rican, that his name was Pedro, that he had this fabulous heavy Spanish accent, and that he was active-duty military and would only be here for the next two weeks. I told her how he'd written his number on a napkin and left it at my seat while I had been dancing. I told her that normally I would've thrown the napkin away, but instead, I'd held on to it. I told her how I'd sent the text, nervous and reluctant, laboring over what to write, wondering if he'd even reply. I explained that he'd texted me back and was polite and enthusiastic and eager to see me again.

She said she didn't mind, but she said it with a side-eyed glance. Ever the protector, Farren knew my history of growing too attached, loving too soon, too much—especially with guys who turned out to be assholes. She'd been the voice of reason, echoing my mother's concerns, when I giddily announced my engagement to a man twenty-five years my senior. After that marriage ended in divorce in 2014, she'd been the first to sound alarms about rekindling a relationship with an ex-boyfriend who'd gained himself an unpopular reputation and was still in his own failing marriage at the time. She'd always been right. And even though I hadn't mentioned love or anything close to it, she was aware of my susceptible nature and ever-opened heart. I imagined it was one of the reasons she'd loved me all these years, but it was that same porous heart that rendered me in need of her protection.

Pedro arrived at the bar with two friends. I wasn't sure if he'd recognize me minus the ripped jeans, disco ball, hypnotic salsa rhythms, and low lights. But he did. He spotted me right away. I didn't even have to wave to catch his attention. He kissed me on the cheek when he greeted me, as if we'd known each other for more than twenty-four hours, as if we were old friends. He wore a khaki baseball cap, a large-faced Fossil wristwatch, and an infectious smile. The sleeves on his turquoise polo hugged his biceps in a way that made him far more attractive than he had appeared the night before. For me, his presence was a shot of espresso—the same color as his eyes.

The three men sat down with us, scooting into the booths and pulling up a chair. After exchanging introductions and obligatory pleasantries, they ordered drinks. The conversation took a purposefully adult tone. Being two single mothers approaching forty, Farren and I clamored for moments when we could speak freely without having to censor ourselves because kids were in earshot. We mocked local talentless strip clubs, teased Pedro for his old-school yet winning approach, played the guess-how-old-I-am game (at thirty-seven, it turned out I was the oldest), and discussed the misunderstood value of bourbon. All three of the men were soldiers and quite candid about not wanting to discuss the army. "I usually just tell people I work for the government and leave it at that. Then I don't have to deal with the questions about where I'm stationed and what I do," confessed the light-eyed fellow sitting next to Farren.

Feeling the need to restore a lighter mood, I changed the topic to the previous night. I joked about how bad a dancer I had been, partly because I felt it to be true, partly because I wanted to appear self-effacing and humble in front of Pedro. Seated in the booth next to me, he protested, "No, no! I think you are a pretty good dancer." It was then that I noticed his faint freckles and deep dimples and caught the scent of his cologne—a refined and stately elixir. His returning gaze flattered me for no reason, until a silver flash from his right index finger gave me pause. I thought to myself, *Could that be a wedding ring? On his right hand?*

Without reflecting my interior panic, I casually posed a question to the group. "So, are y'all single?"

Everyone replied "yes" or "divorced" except for Pedro. He hesitated, perhaps only for a full four seconds. But it felt like a lifetime to me, waiting either to give in to whimsy or be sobered by a single blow. Just above a whisper, Pedro admitted, "I'm . . . married." The look on Farren's face was half horror, half knew-it-all-along. The looks on his friends' faces were a mix between *What the fuck are you thinking!* and *You idiot!* I don't know how my own expression read, but I felt defeated. Pedro's demeanor diminished as he tried a number of tired justifications: "I'm being honest. My wife will never find out. Let me pose a hypothetical question: Even if I had said that I was single, I'm still only here for two weeks. What difference would it have made?" By this point, I was annoyed and offended, though I wasn't mad.

I asked Pedro how long he'd been married. Seven years. I asked him why'd he even leave his number for me. He didn't know. That was a lie. Maybe he didn't want to say it to me, but I got the sense that he didn't want to say it to himself. I knew exactly why he'd scribbled his number on that napkin because I knew exactly what it was to be thirty-three and married seven years. The hankering. The pressure. The dread. The mundanity. The tightening of the chest that happens every time you contemplate the next twenty years of your life. The incessant fear that you are no longer the person you were on your wedding day. The realization that love had only been the starter emotion. The yearning to know what might have been, to know if you've still got that proverbial "it." Asking the question was useless. Then I asked Pedro if this was his habit—reporting to various duty stations, picking up women, cheating on his wife. He insisted that he'd never pursued anyone outside of his marriage before. I didn't believe him.

I stared at him until I could discern the black center of his eye from the surrounding deep-brown hue, searching for truth. I shook my head and explained that I'd been involved with a married man the year before and the affair nearly broke me. I told him that I wasn't interested in revisiting anything resembling that experience.

Pedro shrunk and apologized. He seemed chastened by the moment. The men said their goodbyes and nice-to-meet-yous and headed off to a nearby after-hours spot. I gave Pedro a friendly parting embrace and tried to make a joke, advising him to keep his number to himself that night. The awkwardness still lingered as they walked out and started down the block.

Farren and I headed to our cars, dismayed but not surprised. "That's why I don't fuck with niggas! Shit like that!" Farren asserted. I could only agree. As we navigated the busy Saturday-night sidewalk, we lamented our men troubles and spoke frankly about the usefulness of sex toys. We laughed out loud, but I confessed that sometimes I missed the parts of sex that had nothing to do with an orgasm. Sometimes I just craved the comfort and heat of another body—legs entangled with my own, the touch of hands that didn't belong to me. The night seemed to be a bust. Farren and I hugged before we got into our vehicles.

Before cranking up my car, I checked my phone. A modern-day habit, I suppose. There were three text messages from Pedro. The first was another apology. The second was a compliment, saying that I had looked lovely in white. The third was a message telling me where they ended up, only a few blocks away—a subtle suggestion that he was still interested despite my reaction. Without the shield of Farren's glare and judgement, I was defenseless. Human, insecure, and in need of validation and warmth no matter how fleeting or artificial, I slowly typed that he needn't be sorry. I told him I was free on Monday and Wednesday of the coming week. He replied that he'd call on Wednesday.

Sunday, June 18, 2017

I wondered if Pedro was a father.

It seemed like a reasonable expectation for a man in his early thirties who'd been married seven years. I wondered if he'd talked to his probable daughter or son, if they'd missed their dad on Father's Day, if they'd

FaceTimed him, if they had dark eyes like his, if they spoke Spanish, if they called him Papa instead of Daddy, if they were even old enough to talk, if they even existed.

Tuesday, June 20, 2017

Me: Are we still planning to see each other tomorrow? Just making sure so I can clear my schedule.

Pedro: Of course, I'm planning to see you tomorrow. It's all up to you.

Me: Sounds good. Call me when you're done for the day and we'll connect from there. Just me and you.

Pedro: Alright. I'll call you tomorrow. Just me and you.

Wednesday, June 21, 2017

It was the unknowns that undid me at first. I wondered what kind of car he drove while I shaved my legs. In the shower, I fretted over all the rumors I'd heard about Latino men: they're hot-headed, they're notorious lovers, they're a little unhinged. Simultaneously, I patted concealer over the dark circles under my eyes and worried if Pedro would turn out to be obstinate and arrogant like other service members I'd known. As I sprayed a mist of Cool Water through my hair, it occurred to me that it was possible he wouldn't even call. He could still choose to do the right thing. Not wanting to ruin my makeup, I fanned my eyes to keep them from filling with tears when I realized that I had the exact same choice. Then my phone rang.

"Hey!" I answered, masking my nerves and guilty conscious with forced cheer.

"Hi!" he replied, his cheer sounding more genuine than mine. "So, have you had dinner yet?"

"No. Do you have anywhere in mind?"

"Umm, how about Cheddar's?"

"That's perfect. I can meet you there by 6:45."

"I can pick you up."

"I don't mind driving. I'll meet you there."

"Okay. I'll see you in a few."

I hung up the phone relieved, thankful that he hadn't insulted me by insinuating sex from the outset. He was just as willing to treat this encounter like a real date as I was. His inclination to pretend was a small mercy.

The drive to Cheddar's felt quicker than it should've. Every light was green, and I arrived with two minutes to spare. When I walked in, I found that Pedro had already put us on the list to be seated. He greeted me with the same bright smile, the same kiss on the cheek, the same friendly embrace. It being a Wednesday night, we were seated almost immediately. I ordered the first of two Painkillers, the strongest cocktail on the beverage menu. Pedro opted for glasses of Riesling. Alcohol seemed like the appropriate companion for sitting on the cusp of willful sin. The fact that I was even there with him was a surrender, a concession speech declaring my frustration with the dating universe, my failure to attract monogamy. This was the fourth date I'd been on in the three years since my divorce was finalized, and it was imaginary at best. Showing up on this night had been the epitome of *Fuck it*.

The one upside to this virtual date was that there were no blinders, none of the routine pretension that comes with the effort to impress an individual. In fact, it was stark honesty that would best define these moments with Pedro. He confessed that he'd considered lying about his marital status before telling the truth. I conceded that he had made the best choice. We didn't linger on the obvious. We relaxed, leaned in, listened, laughed.

Pedro described himself as "a conservative, but not a Trump voter." I rolled my eyes but heard him out. He'd voted for Marco Rubio in the primary for reasons not much different than mine when I voted for Barack Obama in 2008. I told him about my past life as a congressional staffer and begrudgingly admitted that Clinton's campaign had been flawed. I asked Pedro, other than dancing, what he did for fun. He wavered a bit before saying that most of his free time was spent with his two kids, five and seven, a boy and a girl. He bit his bottom lip as a veil of concern began to fill his expression. Pedro seemed to think that the revelation of children might morally sober me, make me a less willing participant in this ruse. He was visibly relieved when I told him I had two boys, ten and seventeen. I waxed poetic about my hatred for ideals placed on pedestals—marriage, religion, order. He was struck when I revealed that both my parents were dead and that both had died young—father at forty-four, mother at fifty-five. He managed the lighter side of the conversation, recounting the rowdy and embarrassing behavior of his colleagues at the nightclub on the night we met, complaining about being micromanaged at work, contemplating the appeal of tattoos and the woes of being the baby boy in a family full of girls. I finished the last sip of my second drink as I glanced at my phone and realized that nearly two hours had passed.

God hates me. Pedro had been smart and articulate and funny and thoughtful and decisive. I sincerely wanted to be alone with this man. For every voice in my head (mainly Farren's) that was telling me to thank him for the drinks and truly engaging discussion, race to my car, speed home, grab the vibrator from the nightstand, and take a long shower, there was a louder voice singing the lyrics to Donny Hathaway's "For All We Know." Donny's argument that tomorrow may never come crushed the vibrator, hands down.

"I've got somewhere I want to show you," I said as we got up to leave the table. I opted to ride with him while offering directions from the passenger seat. After about a ten-minute drive, we pulled up in the parking lot of what probably appeared to be a park. We got out of the car, and I grabbed his wrist. "C'mon." I felt like a nine-year-old with a secret hiding place.

We made our way down a semisteep incline toward a wooded path. "It's so nice out here," Pedro commented, admiring the landscape as it sunk deeper into twilight.

"It gets better." I smiled. It was the summer solstice, the longest day of the year, and at a little after 9:00 p.m. we still had a sliver of sun. Above us, generous bits of a pink sunset peeked through a canopy of trees draped in Spanish moss. Pedro slid his fingers between mine as we approached a small clearing. On the other side of the clearing, a staircase led us up to the headgate where the Augusta Canal rushes out to the Savannah River. The roar of the rapids grew louder as we strolled closer to our destination. We climbed one last short set of steps before we found ourselves looking out over the rushing water, black as sin, the sun finally shrouded behind a sky awash in deep indigos and violets.

"Wow!" Pedro was dumbfounded. He'd never imagined a gem like this in an unremarkable city that only boasted two-star strippers and one halfway decent Latin nightspot. He looked at me as though I were brilliant. "It's so peaceful out here. Do you come out here to write?"

"Sometimes. I mainly come here to think."

I wondered if he knew what I was thinking right then—that I was on the best date I'd been on in my entire life and it was with an unavailable man, that this moment was just as hopeless as it was poignant. That was when he noticed the three dozen or so padlocks attached to the iron railing. Some were professionally engraved with dates and names while others had sets of initials carved into them. He asked me what they meant. I told him they were love locks like the ones on the Pont des Arts bridge in Paris. I told him that people often came up there to get engaged and make other horrible decisions. We both laughed. Then we were silent—moonlit and fluid like the water beneath us. Pedro put his arm around me, and I laid my head on his shoulder and let tears fill my eyes until I thought he might feel one land on his shirt. The kiss was inevitable.

Strolling back to the car, we swung our clasped hands like kids. Pedro confessed, "I wish I would have met you earlier."

I shook my head. "No. Had we met earlier, it would've been harder to watch you leave," I said, gently reminding him that he only had a few days before he headed back to Texas, where he was stationed.

He opened the passenger door for me and I slid into the seat more conflicted than I'd been at the beginning of the night. The sound of his closing door locked the two of us in with all our awkwardness and longing and unsaid words. Pedro put his left hand on the steering wheel and rested his right hand on mine. He was nervous. Unable to retreat to either a barracks bustling with nosy roommates or a house with two teenaged boys and a disgruntled ex-husband stuck watching them, we decided to get a hotel room. We both were adamant about staying in a hotel, not a motel, even if we only had a few hours.

He took me back to my car and I followed him to a Holiday Inn. I expected that he'd give me cash and ask me to book the room with my credit card, a tried and true married-man strategy to keep suspicions at bay. Instead, we entered the lobby and approached the front desk together. He slid his Visa card from his wallet without even thinking twice. When the lady behind the desk (who I'm sure had her judgments, checking in a bagless pair after 10:00 p.m.) asked for an email address to send the receipt to, a flash of realization filled Pedro's expression like a bucket of cold water had been poured on his head. As the lady stared, he prompted me to offer my email address. As I slowly repeated my email for the lady, I began to believe his insistence that he'd never cheated before. The hotel receipt could give me access to information that no seasoned cheater wants his lover to ever know—his home address, credit card number, full legal name. *What was he thinking?* The lady handed him the keys and we took the elevator to the third floor.

When we stepped into the room, Pedro darted into the bathroom. I kicked off my sandals but kept my dress on and hopped onto the bed— more casual and less come-hither. Pedro emerged from the bathroom fully clothed. He took off his hat and shoes and wristwatch. At first, Pedro was fun and passionate, slipping my dress above my head, his mouth roaming from my lips to my neck to my breasts, tonguing my nipples and the folds between my thighs. I imagined him to be the stereotypical Latin lover that women fantasize about. Finally shirtless, Pedro flipped me onto my stomach. I heard the zipper of his jeans and I reached over to my purse.

"Wait, baby. We need a condom," I insisted, pulling a Trojan from my wallet.

"A condom? I haven't used a condom in years," Pedro replied with nervous laughter, no longer the Latino love machine that he'd been just moments before.

"Well, you have to with me," I asserted, pushing the small foil package into his palms.

With my belly pressed against the overbleached hotel linens, Pedro kissed my back, rubbed my ass, and slid his fingers inside of me. In between moans of "Mmm, baby" and "Damn, you're fine," I heard fumbling. And then silence. Pedro flopped down on the bed next to me, exasperated. Tossing the still unused condom on the floor, he declared, "It isn't working." Was the nonfunctioning "it" his dick? Or his attempt at infidelity? Or both?

I wanted to comfort him, put him at ease. Masculinity is so fragile. A man spends years, even decades, building it up, and it's torn down in mere seconds. Frustrated, Pedro turned his back to me. I ran my fingers across the large swath of salmon-colored skin from his shoulder to his waist and whispered, "It's okay." I felt as If I'd broken him. Like a kid in a toy store who picks up a doll from the shelf, handles her, twists her, turns her, and suddenly, the doll's arm pops off. The kid tries to pop the plastic limb back into its place, but it's too late. The doll is damaged. The kid just walks away, hoping that no one witnessed the crime.

After a few tense minutes passed, Pedro rolled over and pulled me into his chest, ran the tips of his fingers across the surface of my bare back and waist and hips, and I realized that it hadn't been the sex that we sought. It had been the time, the sheer intimacy, the quiet, the darkness, the knowing that the person lying next to you wanted to be in your presence, to share this space with you. There was no second attempt. We were satisfied. We fell asleep facing each other.

I roused myself around 5:00 a.m. and kissed Pedro goodbye. In the car on the way home I decided to lie about this night—not for my sake, but for Pedro's. When Farren asked, I'd tell her that we fucked all night and that he was amazing. Make him sound like a porn star. I didn't care if she thought I was a whore; she knows all my flaws anyway. But there was something about Pedro's tenderness. I felt an obligation to protect his machismo, his reputation as a man. When I arrived at home, I showered, climbed into my own bed, laid my head on the pillow, and finally let the tears flow.

Thursday, June 22, 2017

An inbox alert lights up my phone. It reads, "Pedro ———, Thank you for your stay at the Holiday Inn at ———" I delete it immediately.

Friday, June 23, 2017

Once you've slept with a man who's only in town for a few days, you'd be foolish to expect to hear from him again.

Saturday, June 24, 2017

Pedro: I hope you are having a good time in DC. Be safe!

Me: I am! The ordination service was really nice. I think I'll be back a little earlier than expected tomorrow. Do you want to catch a movie tomorrow night?

Pedro: Sure, we can go to the movies. What movie would you like to watch? Have you seen *Wonder Woman*?

Me: I haven't. That works for me.

Pedro: Okay. I'll see you tomorrow.

Me: Looking forward to it.

Sunday, June 25, 2017

I'd forgotten that I'd mentioned traveling to my brother's ordination when Pedro's text lit up my phone on Saturday night. I was both surprised and heartened. It'd made the eight-hour drive back to Georgia less dreadful. I arrived at home with just enough time to take a nap, wake up, and pull myself together for another faux date. This time there were fewer unknowns, even fewer nerves, and I let him pick me up.

I hopped into the car happier than I wanted to let on, trying not to let my smile morph into an official grin. I wasn't worried about Pedro noticing my excitement, I just didn't want that excitement to be mistaken for true attachment. I didn't want him to feel like he'd have to worry about me calling him in the middle of his son's karate lessons, or me sending him a stupid-ass nude selfie via text at two in the morning, or that I would even attempt to communicate with him at all after he left. He needed the comfort of knowing that my joy was for this moment and nothing beyond.

He asked an unanticipated question as we pulled out of my subdivision onto the main road. "What do your sons think about you dating?" I was taken aback but pleased that he asked about my kids. I told him the truth—that the oldest seemed glad to see me getting out and enjoying myself, but the ten-year-old was more suspicious. Whenever I returned home from a date or night out with friends, he behaved like a jealous husband or overprotective father, peppering me with questions while he wore a disapproving scowl. Pedro chuckled and said that it was sweet that my son showed so much concern. Then he told me how his daughter called him every day, demanding a detailed account of every minute of every hour. He grinned as he spoke about her, imitating her five-year-old voice. I heard the longing in the back of his throat, the *I miss my daughter, I miss my family, I miss home*. That's when I started to miss him.

The beauty of expiration dates is that we can prepare accordingly. We can pad the unavoidable hits, steel ourselves for the inescapable stings. We waste nothing—not a word, not a second, not a kind glance, not a reassuring pat on the back, not a gentle squeeze of the palm, not a single merciful gesture. A keen awareness of the coming dusk makes the hours in the daylight so much more precious.

Pedro interrupted my swelling affection. "You know, I could never live in Augusta." As if to say, *Even if I could love you (which I cannot), I could never love you here*. He took his eyes off the road briefly, scanning my face for a reaction. I looked back at him, pretending not to have heard what he didn't say.

"I don't think I'll be here forever," I replied, feeling a new kind of terror at the thought of forever.

"I don't meet many people who have lived in one place all their life."

I shouldn't have taken his comment personally, but I did. My cheeks burned. I was envious and embarrassed for having been so sedentary, so married to this city. I thought about the places he'd been—Iraq, Afghanistan, Greece—and the range of his experiences—the unconditional love of family, the unforgiving violence of war—and I felt small and unbrave. I only spoke one language, lived in one place. When we arrived at the theater, I was thankful that the next 120 minutes would be marked by silence. I'd been humbled enough for one day, perhaps for a lifetime.

Tuesday, June 27, 2017

Me: If you don't have other plans, you should let me treat you to dinner this evening (one of your last meals here). I should finish up around 7:00 p.m. Let me know if you're interested.

Pedro: I would love to go out with you, but that won't be possible tonight. Maybe we can plan for tomorrow night.

Me: Okay. I'll look to hear from you tomorrow.

Wednesday, June 28, 2017

Pedro: Hi, Kristie. I haven't called because I'm still at school waiting for the instructors to release us. They decided to close everything out tonight so we can leave early tomorrow morning.

Me: No worries.

What I didn't say: I'm cooking pasta with Italian sausage and a red wine sauce because that's what I do when I'm sad. I pour a glass of something strong (Malibu and cranberry juice or the merlot that I use in my sauce) and listen to music while the sausage browns and fettucine boils. Tonight, I put on Carl Thomas and when "I Wish" came on (*and I wish I never met her at all*), I thought about you. I cried, then I laughed when I remembered something that a friend said about me many years ago. Farren had asked me why I'd never written poems about her and before I could answer, another friend replied to her abruptly, "You gotta tongue kiss her!" We'd laughed so hard. But it had been a bit true. I save poems for deep, inexpressible connections—the things that we feel but dare not speak into existence. I can't tell you that I believe you now. I believe that you're a guy who loves his family and just lost his way for a moment. I can't tell you how your choosing to treat me like a complete human rather than a set of sex organs has renewed my faith in the goodness of people, especially men. I can't tell you that now I'm beginning to understand that when you said you wished you'd met me earlier, you didn't mean earlier during your time in Augusta; you meant earlier in life, before the army, before the wife, before the kids, before this lifetime. I can't tell you how, in just a week's time, you've inspired me to make my world bigger, expanding beyond Georgia and the borders of the US. I can't tell you that I don't want to never see you again. So, I'll put it on the page, in bright cerulean ink, two poems, maybe even three, and, in time, I'll be okay.

Thursday, June 29, 2017

Me: Hey, I just wanted to let you know that I said a prayer for you this morning. I wish you safe travels and success in everything that lies ahead for you. Take care of yourself.

Pedro: Thank you for the kind words. I had an outstanding time and I wish the same for you. Take care!

Things don't always end badly. Sometimes, they just end.

The Cookie Man

When the polished black Tundra backed into the parking space in front of the barbershop, meticulous and slow, the driver making sure not to get a scratch on the freshly cleaned ride, I thought nothing of it. Another old man getting his hair cut on a busy Saturday morning. But the reaction of everyone in the shop taught me otherwise. Before the man could place his vehicle in park, a stir of excitement spread through the small brick building. Two barbers hastily dropped their clippers and my own stylist yelled across the room to her coworker, "Hey B, the Cookie Man is here!" as she pulled her hands from my head full of crocheted curls to grab her purse.

"Who is the Cookie Man?" I asked, beginning to feel the contagion of frenzy bubble in my own spirit.

"He stops by every few weeks or so with cookies from the plant," she replied, referencing the President Baking Company on Augusta's south side. The plant manufactures products for Nabisco.

"He's got some good deals?"

"Yes, girl. C'mon!"

Not even bothering to remove the purple cape secured around my neck to keep hair off my clothes, I snatched up my purse and followed her out the front door. My eleven-year-old, Patrick, followed me. About six or seven of us gathered in the parking lot, forming an imperfect semicircle around the truck's flatbed, our reflections staring back at us, as clear as any mirror. Without cutting off the engine, the middle-aged black man lifted the cover of the flatbed to reveal an array of sweets that rivaled that of any grocery store aisle. My son's face expanded like an orange sunrise and his eyes darted from one bright color to the next: golden packages of belVita Breakfast Biscuits and Nilla Wafers, shiny blue bags of Teddy Grahams and Chips Ahoy and Oreos, cardinal-colored boxes of Ritz Crackers and Nutter Butters and Barnum's Animal Crackers. Pointing to different sections of items, the man explained, "These packs are one dollar, the twelve-pack boxes are two dollars, the thirty-pack boxes are five dollars, and the individual bags right here are twenty-five cents apiece." There was no lingering or haggling. We made our selections swiftly, exchanged crumpled bills and coins found in the ashtrays of our cars or the lint-filled bottoms of our handbags, and within minutes the Cookie Man was off to his next stop. My prize: a five-dollar thirty-pack assortment of Oreos, Chips Ahoys, and animal crackers that I would've normally paid twelve dollars for at the Costco, ten dollars if they were on sale. Patrick's prize: a one-dollar package of chocolate, double-stuffed Oreos that would've been almost five dollars at our local Kroger, and a bonus two-dollar twelve-count box of individual Oreo six-packs that his barber purchased for him out of sheer delight at Patrick's amazement (the same reason adults enjoy Christmas Day long after they've stopped believing in Santa).

As we headed home, already under the spell of a preemptive sugar high from all the cookies he planned to eat, Patrick asked, "Where'd he get all those cookies?"

Herein lies the essential paradox of parenthood: We wish to raise flawless creatures as we live flawed lives in a vastly flawed world. The task is impossible, yet we strive. And just when we think we're getting it right, here comes the Cookie Man.

I could've lied and said that President Baking was a generous employer and gave all their employees surplus products at the end of each quarter. But I chose the more difficult path and told him the truth. I stumbled my way through a complicated, but honest, explanation. I told him that, more than likely, the Cookie Man works at the plant and has access to products that, for some reason, don't end up on shelves in the grocery store. He had probably devised a system for getting the packages from the plant to his car to his home, and when he accumulates an abundance, he sells them. Before Patrick could ask, I told him it was illegal, that if the Cookie Man ever got caught selling the treats, he could go to jail. I also explained that we could've gotten in trouble for buying the cookies as well. I half expected my child to be scared straight, appalled that I'd allowed him to take part in a crime. Then I remembered that he is my child, and he thrives upon candor, justice, and rebellion just like his mother. He only cries when he feels he's being lied about or being lied to. He's spent countless hours in the back seat of my Hyundai devouring Nas's *Illmatic*, Kanye West's *The College Dropout*, J. Cole's *Born Sinner*, and more recently Jay-Z's *4:44* along with anything by Kendrick Lamar. He's spent the whole of his short life listening to black men lament a rigged system. He's watched his own father work upwards of fifty hours a week as a car salesman and still not make enough money to keep his own vehicle from being repossessed. Eleven years on this planet had presented him with all the evidence he needed to understand that the Cookie Man is more Robin Hood and less Al Capone. His only reply was, "Oh. Okay," as he popped a contraband mini-Oreo into his mouth.

That visit to the barbershop took me back to my own upbringing and all the veritable "cookie men" that I'd come to know and even admire. Both of my childhood homes—my mother's house and my grandmother's house—had been situated in areas that many would describe as the hood. People often talk about the so-called hood like it's something from which one must escape—like Alcatraz, Nazi Germany, or bad relationships. The truth is the notion of the hood isn't something that can be readily defined. It's not a redlined, forty-block section in the dark heart of Chicago's South Side or the notorious SWAT section of Atlanta. It's not a ten-story housing project replete with broken windows, malfunctioning elevators, chipped flakes of lead paint, and rodents holding families with failing lungs dying slow like their dreams. It's not a suburban neighborhood that used to gleam with manicured lawns and pink faces with pearly-white grins until the undesirables moved in with their brown, black, and yellow faces and their cornrows and dreadlocks, and their indecipherable native tongues. It's not bass-laden rap music, booming from Impalas and lowriders. It's not baby daddies and baby mamas, or grannies and abuelitas, or credit scores below six hundred, or mangled renditions of "The Star-Spangled Banner." It is not every place that white people have deemed dangerous, nor is it any heretical version of what it means to be an American. The hood is really a state of mind—and a glorious one at that.

The hood experience not only made me streetwise and cautious, it also taught me an unfathomable tenderness and generosity. The hood is five single mothers who live on the same block coming together to throw a rent party for one of their own when she gets laid off from her second part-time job. The hood is grandmas and aunties putting up their houses—their most valuable worldly possessions—to post bail for grandsons and nephews who are guilty but misunderstood. The hood is the apostle Paul's version of love: bearing all things, believing all things, hoping all things, enduring all things. The Cookie Man reminded me of the seemingly wanton risk-takers of my youth and the impact they had on my worldview.

First, we met the Water Man. I must have been in my early teens, freshman year of high school, perhaps. I don't remember much about the day we met him except that it was hot. I do, however, remember his face. It was the roundest face I'd ever seen—a perfect circle, the same color as a honey bun. It had to have been at least ninety degrees that day, and the Water Man was walking from house to house reading meters. His stride was ardent but slowing. My grandmother must have noticed, because she offered him a cool drink as he approached our yard. She poured him a tall glass of ice water, and he swallowed the whole thing in one gulp while standing in our driveway. He happily handed the empty glass back to my grandmother, his smile on the verge of laughter. He and my grandmother swapped small talk about the heat and high utility prices. After that day, I only remember seeing him checking meters in the neighborhood two or three more times. But I do recall—because one of my tasks was to help my grandmother write out checks for her bills each month—that our monthly water bill never exceeded ten dollars after we met the Water Man. The bill would've normally been around twenty-five dollars. It seemed that we'd received that most precious of cultural commodities known as a hookup. And this wouldn't be the last.

We once met an overworked cable installation man who also happened to be a distant cousin, and he gifted us with free HBO for nearly two years. When I was a senior in high school, we met the Dress Lady—a tall, slim fair-skinned black woman with bewitching green eyes and a cropped haircut. She was a friend of our next-door neighbor. It turned out she had a talent for shoplifting high-end garments. She'd hit up the Talbots and Ann Taylor stores on the other side of town and sell the pieces from the back of her trunk. Much like the Cookie Man, she'd appear and disappear within minutes. In later years, we discovered the Movie Guy, better known as the Bootleg Man. He pirated movies that were still in the theaters from the internet, downloaded them onto blank DVDs, and sold them for five dollars a pop. By the letter of the law, each was a criminal.

But for those of us who were in precarious economic situations, each was a kind of unholy miracle. My grandmother saved 180 dollars thanks to the Water Man. She used that money to help send me on a trip to Orlando with the high school chorus. Cable television may seem like a nominal necessity of modern life, but for us it was a true extravagance to pop popcorn in our secondhand microwave, snuggle up on the couch, and take in a movie. And the dresses that my mother got from the Dress Lady lifted my chin a bit, made me feel worthy, and saved me a few days of having to show up to school in hand-me-downs and knockoffs.

And though the Water Man, the Dress Lady, the Cable Guy, and the Bootleg Man never spoke openly about what plagued us all, we knew why they did what they did. Money and survival are the easy pop psychology answers. To examine what really lies beneath one's willingness to break the law—to risk their freedom—for what seems to be such insignificant gain requires an intimate understanding of oppression. While the Water Man and Cable Guy were both gainfully employed citizens, they both understood that they were rare exceptions to a savage rule. African American men are twice as likely as white men to suffer sustained unemployment. They didn't need degrees in economics to understand the wealth gap. They'd lived the disparity. They'd attended schools with white classmates whose moms had only one job or didn't work at all while their mothers had worked two and three jobs at a time just to break even. And the Dress Lady and the Bootleg Man—outright thieves—knew what it was to be priced out of the American Dream, to be the offspring of grandparents and great-grandparents who tilled and ploughed land only to have the products they worked to harvest swindled from them, to pay double the price for the near-rotting fruits and vegetables shipped into their neighborhoods under the guise of convenience. Their toothless insurrections were—in many ways—acts of vengeance, their crude way of achieving some semblance of comeuppance in a patently unfair system.

About a month after the encounter with the Cookie Man, I sat at the foot of Aunt Edna's bed. Aunt Edna is an older dear friend who has been my surrogate mother since my real mother passed away. And I've never told her this, but she is the most beautiful human I've ever seen. Her profile is Nefertiti. Face forward, she is Cleopatra bathed in black sand. Her coffee-colored skin smooths across her five-foot-eight-inch frame as though it's been poured on. Her eyes slant upward when she smiles, accentuating sharp cheekbones and small, but plump, lips. She never needs to wear makeup and, when she does, it's impossible not to stare or to feel diminished by her regality. I've known Aunt Edna since I was six years old, and she's worked in cosmetics and retail most of her life. Even though she's always earned an hourly wage, she seemed to live a lavish life that was always out of my reach. The first time I ever saw a bottle of Dom Pérignon that wasn't in a magazine ad or a rapper's video was on Aunt Edna's kitchen countertop. I once spied a 750-dollar price tag on a shoebox in her closet. As a young girl, it never occurred to me that the math didn't add up. While Aunt Edna was certainly sumptuous, she'd never been rich. Aunt Edna was, at this time, near retirement age but needed to continue working to make ends meet. She'd undergone two surgeries in the previous six months. She was weaker, but still stunning.

During this visit, she asked me about my kids, how they were doing in school, how I was doing in school. She ran down the list of all her current medications, bragged on her own two grandchildren. As with all our conversations, especially since my mother's death, she said that she was proud of me, that she loved me. Just before standing up to leave, I remembered the cash in my back pocket.

"You come across anything good lately?" I asked.

"Pull out that box right there," she replied, gesturing toward the floor of her closet.

I slid a white shoebox from underneath the stack. It contained bright baubles full of fine colognes and perfumes. I examined the merchandise delicately, as if I were at the fragrance counter at Nordstrom, squirting small aromatic puffs into the air until I inhaled a grassy, citrus scent that I liked. I turned to Aunt Edna. "How much for this one?"

"Thirty-five."

I slid two trifolded twenty-dollar bills from my hand into hers. "Thank you, baby," she half-moaned, leaning over to put the money in her handbag. The exchange was technically illegal, but it was not illicit. We were saving each other's lives in some small way. She was giving me a slice of a world that I'd probably never know, a designer fragrance that would allow me to be equal, for once, to the other tennis moms and the ladies on the opposite side of the interview table. They'd ask, *What are you wearing?* and I'd reply, *Chanel*, in my best Grey Poupon voice, as though it were obvious, and then they'd know that I deserved to be one of them. The two twenties, for my aunt, were a temporary relief—the intended outcome of all hustles. I imagine that the money went toward a past-due medical bill or her grandson's sparse college fund or a mani-pedi. Where I come from, this is how we take care of each other. This is community.

Kristie Robin Johnson

Keep Living

Dear Tine,

That's how I address you now—Tine, no longer Granny. I'm no longer the doting granddaughter, shy and people pleasing. I'm not your Pumpkin begging you to sing a song, to paint and hide Easter eggs in the dead of winter, to drink coffee even after you've told me hundreds of times that it will make me literally black, to not hit me with the extension cord. I'm a woman now, like you—fearless, gritty, and hurting. We don't have time for frivolous pleasantries. We are broke, but never broken. We work harder than anyone could ever pay us to work. We love harder than anyone could ever love us back. We're weapons, chiseled out of the granite mountains of lifetimes filled with loss. Too often we slice into the softest parts of others. Most often we cut ourselves. We're irreverent and vulgar. We curse too much. We say *pussy*, *fuck*, and *dick*. We drink beer from the can, Crown Royal from the bottle, and eat civility for breakfast. We're beautiful, rare, brown-skinned gems, raised barefoot by women with hearts of concrete. That's who we are, you and me.

If you were here today, I imagine you'd find yourself in my family room, resting comfortably on the love seat, squinting at the flat screen, watching whatever is on, wearing an invisible smile. Or in the far end of my backyard (miniscule in comparison to yours), folded into a downward facing dog, pulling weeds from the earth, protected by a flimsy muumuu and a wide-brimmed straw hat. Or better yet, you'd be at my stove, hot comb in hand, pressing my hair one last time, for old times' sake. I can almost feel the sting of hot bergamot grease meeting my freshly cleaned scalp. If you were here, you'd scoot your bifocals down the bridge of your nose, raise a presumptuous eyebrow, and say, "I guess you think you're stepping in high cotton now?" I'd respectfully reply, "No ma'am," feeling small and timid again like your Pumpkin, all the while knowing that this is high cotton to you. You were born in Lincolnton and raised on a farm and your grandparents were oft-swindled sharecroppers and your great-grandparents were slaves. Even after you had worked thirty years for the Army and Air Force Exchange and purchased your own home, you still cleaned white folks' houses to make ends meet, to give me some small luxury that you didn't have as a child—a swing set, a new bicycle, a house with an air conditioning unit. So yes, a two-story home with a two-car garage and central heat and air in the middle of suburbia is, indeed, high cotton.

I'm not sure why this is my first attempt in fourteen years to break through that impermeable plane between life and whatever lies beyond it, but here I am. I guess I am writing to you because I owe you a debt, and it seems impossible to pay a debt to a ghost. Most people hang pictures, visit graves, even post some old photo and kind words on Facebook to remember their kin. I do not. I've built no shrines. I haven't hung a single picture of you or Mama Zula or Auntie Lillie or my mother or my father in my home. Nor do I visit any of your graves. I didn't even bother burying my mother because I knew that I'd never return to that soulless hole in the ground. I had her cremated and she (well, her remains) rode home in the car with me when we left the funeral home. Somehow, that act felt less dire, less final. Remembrance, for me, is less an act of worshipping inanimate artifacts—photographs, gravestones, pictures on T-shirts, flowers in memoriam—and more of an act that resides in the soul and mind. I don't need to gaze at your photos because I see your wide grin, flattened nose, slanted eyes every time I dare to smile at myself, posing for a godforsaken selfie. I see fragments of your presence in Bobby when he's standing alone, lost in his thoughts, the heel of his right foot resting on the inside of his left thigh just above the knee. Balancing with one-legged grace, the lower half of him twisted into a tan figure four, capturing the African elegance of the pose you'd struck so many times standing at your sink cleaning collards for a Sunday dinner. I see flashes of you in Patrick, my baby who was born after you died, every summer afternoon when he rushes outside to worship the sun, wriggle his toes in blades of striking green grass, study the dirt, examine creatures small enough to stand on the tip of his curious finger, bask in nature—a habit he, no doubt, inherits from you. I relish your face the most on nights that I am lucky enough to dream about you in color, to revisit that small green house in the cul-de-sac, to which I never return during my waking hours. Sometimes in these dreams you offer wise and comforting words. Other times you just hum a familiar soothing hymn, fixing everything in your own peculiar fashion. In this way, you exist despite your death.

Of all the things you gave me, there is one phrase, one simple redundant reply that you often offered to some of my most complex questions, and it anchors me to your spirit to this day. I'd ask, "Granny, how can you say he's up to no good when you don't even know him?" or, "How do you remain so faithful to a god who allows terrible things to happen to you?" Without raising your voice or flinching in reaction to my blasphemous audacity, you just chuckled lightly through a satisfied smile and said, "Keep living, baby. Keep living." Whether I was six, seventeen, or twenty-one, the answer remained the same. The simplicity and mystery of this answer frustrated me for many years. In my youth, I thought it was a cop-out—a quick way to get rid of a pesky kid. As I grew older, I understood better but lacked the patience to achieve your level of peace with a chaotic and uncertain world. So, I took your advice. I kept living. I saw four police officers beat a black man nearly to death, then get acquitted of all wrongdoing, and an American city burst into flames; I kept living. I flunked out of college; I kept living. I became a nineteen-year-old single mom; I kept living. Together, you and I watched the world tumble off its axis on live television. The split screen showing desperate men and women leaping from the twin towers alongside billowing clouds of smoke flowing from the Pentagon left me reeling and searching for purpose. You kept living.

This advice got me through your passing and the untimely passing of my mother. Both instances left me not wanting to live. At all. But both times, I opened my eyes the next morning, allowed grief-stricken air to fill my lungs, exhaled, and kept living.

You died less than twelve hours into your first day in hospice. The nurse said that it was time, that the death rattles had begun. I thought it displayed a certain sensitivity on her part to use your comforting colloquialism rather than the clinical terminology: terminal respiratory secretions. By passing slowly, you gave your family the gift of knowing. We had a few precious minutes to gather our thoughts, to rehearse the final moment in our minds. I spent the last minutes rubbing your feet. They were snuggled in a pair of fuzzy blue hospital footies with rubber soles. My mother stood at the head of your bed running her fingers through your hair. With a cascade of tears flowing beneath her chin, she whispered, "It's okay, Tine. You can go." She was inconsolable for weeks.

When my mother died four years later, we weren't granted the gift of knowing. She just went to sleep and never woke up. On that day, I felt closer to you than I ever imagined possible. Staring down at Pat, the truth of our bond became so clear. For decades, we'd carried the invisible burden of loving someone who did not love themself. Pat's struggle with addiction consumed our lives for years. Together we waited for missing cars—usually traded for drugs—to show up. Together we prayed to a formless God in a small church on Eighth Avenue, putting Pat in God's hands, whatever the hell that was supposed to mean. Together we stood in the lobbies of rehabilitation facilities, hoping this detox would be the one that stuck. Together we sat in an Al-Anon meeting feeling like aliens while white people talked about their addict sons, daughters, sisters, brothers, and parents. We decided they were weak, and we never returned. We were so wrong. But we were together. And I think that, somewhere, we were taught that black women don't have the luxury of being victims. We were always survivors and *only* survivors—without license for public tears, admission of hurt feelings, or sharing of our heavy secrets.

In many ways I felt as if I lost a mother and a daughter. I rooted for her recovery like I'd given birth to her myself. I wish I could tell you that she was sober when she passed away. But I don't know. I'll tell you what I do know. I know that she tried very hard to stay clean, but the work of exorcising deep-rooted demons is a daunting and lonely task. I know that there were no signs of drugs or drug paraphernalia in her home, no pipes, no half-crushed Pepsi cans, no empty burnt Tylenol bottles. I know that she didn't suffer that day and will never suffer again. The first time I looked in the mirror after she was gone, I heard your voice just as clear as if you'd materialized from the stark nothingness of the morning. You said, *You look just like your mama,* as I examined the corners of my mouth and the coffee-colored half circles under my eyes. Few moments in life carry such pause as the moment you realize that you are your mother.

A part of me feels silly, like the little girl I keep insisting I'm not anymore, telling you things that you probably already know. You used to say that *the dead have nothing to do with the living.* I disagree. Maybe it was one of those soothing myths humans conjure to survive the awareness of their own mortality. To me it seems that the dead have everything to do with the living. Shadows of you and Pat and everyone else that passed away lingered years after Uncle Ray ate the last piece of fried chicken at the repast. You are an unshakeable, eternal gift. My first thoughts as I welcomed my second child were of the both of you. Would he have your laugh or Mama's penchant for taking risks? Could he ever really know who you were? Who was going to insist upon homespun, magical remedies when he came down with his first cold or started teething? Who was going to burn a needle-sized hole in a penny and slide it on to a turpentine-soaked piece of thread and lay it on his tiny chest to open his congested airways? Who was going to remind me to put an egg in one of his father's socks and hang it over his door to prevent colic when he began to cut teeth? And again, I thought of the two of you first on election night, 2008. A black president. I wasn't worthy. You were the ones who had survived colored-only restrooms, segregated schools, the growing pains of justice delayed. You and everyone who came before you had earned the right to witness that history. I was just a stowaway fattened by your sacrifices, reaping the reward.

Being your daughter's daughter has been an invaluable education in the art of loving and being loved. When I came to you during my sophomore year at Georgia State, head hung in disgrace, and told you I was pregnant, I was embarrassed and remorseful. I had let you down. As disappointed as you were, you rejected my apology. You told me that I didn't owe you anything, that my sole obligation in life was to my unborn child. And six months later you were right there to welcome my firstborn into the world without judgment or a single iota of shame, celebrating me and my baby.

More than anything, having you in my life taught me that it's crucial to surround myself with people who remember my dreams, because the real duty of dreams is to separate a person, almost completely, from all that they know. Dreams, by design, relieve us of our realities and transport us to an existence so indisputably our own that others often fail to recognize it. People who love us enough to remember our dreams don't fret when we disappear. They don't feel abandoned when we stop answering the phone to go back to school or train eight hours a day to run a marathon or open a pet rescue or pen a memoir or adopt a child. No matter how far from home I strayed, you always loved me enough to remember my dreams.

Every day I am startled at how much of you remains in me: the good, the bad, and the complicated. With the heaviest of sighs, I echoed, "Keep living, baby," when my ten-year-old, blinking back tears, questioned the election of Donald Trump; he couldn't grasp the notion that millions of his fellow Americans could be led so far away from the path of progress so willingly. I wake each morning and thank the God that you introduced me to for breath in my body. I talk to God aloud in a hushed, pious voice before streetlamps shut off in favor of the coming light of day. I add a capful of bleach to the water when I wash dishes and I still wash them by hand even though I own a dishwasher. I demand made beds and overtalk friends and am always painfully unaware of my worth. I haven't much patience for laziness nor tolerance for liars, and I have a temper only found in the roiling center of a vipers' nest. I constantly remain in dogged pursuit of respect and reckless pursuit of love. Sometimes the impulse to cry rises in my chest and throat and I can taste the coming sorrow, but I fight it for fear of appearing weak. I reject human frailty, expecting children to endure man-sized pain and grown-ups to never stumble. I am passionate, unreasonable, and most of the time, insecure. And I am grateful, always, for this bloodline of impudence and pain and pride that rushes through my veins. And in your honor, perhaps as the only act that will do justice to your name, I keep living.

Acknowledgments

High Cotton is my first book and my third child, and prayerfully, it will not be my last. And like any offspring, her existence and birth have required far more than the simple, singular ambitions of her mother. It has taken the labor—great and small, visible and invisible, direct and indirect—of family members, friends, colleagues, coworkers, professors, mentors, editors, and publishers to bring this book to life. Following is my humble attempt to thank every individual who had a hand in this creation. If I don't get it right, charge it to the head, not the heart:

MY SOURCE—Jesus Christ, the author and finisher of my faith (and a great deal of the experiences and words in these pages). I thank God for every single day, both the tragic and the triumphant, of my beautiful writable life.

MY EDITOR AND PUBLISHER—Karen Pickell and Raised Voice Press. Thank you for your kindness, generosity, and patience. Thank you for your expertise and advice. Most of all, I thank you for believing in my creative vision.

MY ROOTS—Patricia "Pat" Kennedy Johnson, Robert "Bobby" Johnson (Dad), Christine "Tine" Kennedy, Zula Robinson, and Grady Abrams. You saw my success long before I could imagine being good at anything. Your sacrifices on my behalf have been immeasurable. Till we meet again . . .

MY SUPPORT SYSTEM—Robert "Bobby" Johnson (son), Patrick Gregory, Ken Gregory, and Cheryl Lockett. Thank each of you for graciously giving me the two things that writers need the most: time and space to write. Your sacrifices made putting these words on the page possible. I am forever in your debt.

MY VILLAGE—Guy Johnson, Kimberly Hayes, S'Necka Crawford, Cicely Harpe, Lynthia Ross, Jennifer Branch, Tiffany Stokes, and the extended Johnson/Kennedy/Robinson family. Every prizefighter needs a corner full of loud, tough, honest trainers who will send you back in the ring even when your eye is swollen and ribs are aching because they know you better than you know yourself. I'm so grateful for your words of encouragement, open hearts, and open minds. Y'all kept me in the fight.

THOSE WHO GAVE ME MY FIRST OPPORTUNITIES—Martin Lammon and the Georgia College Master of Fine Arts in Creative Writing Program; the editing teams at *Rigorous, Bloodletters Literary Magazine, HEArt Online, ESME, Split Lip Magazine, Under the Gum Tree, riverSedge,* and *Lunch Ticket*; Ben Hasan and Frederick Benjamin at *Urban Pro Weekly*; and Tiana Ferrell of *Atlanta Free Speech*. Thank you for embracing my work and offering a platform.

MY ADVISORS/TEACHERS—Allen Gee, Peter Selgin, John Sirmans, Laura Newbern, Aubrey Hirsch, Kerry Neville, and Cecilia Woloch. Thank you for never being stingy with your wisdom, criticism, or praise. Most of these essays would not exist if not for your guidance. You've made me a better writer and teacher. I also must mention Laura Caron here. Thank you so much for your support both as a student and graduate.

MY COLLEAGUES/FELLOW WRITERS—Ryan Loveeachother, Noah Devros, Abbie Lahmers, Ernestine Montoya, Roe Sellers, Isabel Acevedo, Jennifer Watkins, Jennifer Watkins (yes, there are two Jennifer Watkinses), Penny Dearmin, Danielle Dicenzo, Ruby Holsenbeck, Georgia Knapp, Mike McClelland, Tara Mettler, Marshall Newman, Ian Sargent, Julia Wagner, Shannon Skelton, George Brannen, Miranda Campbell, Leah Kuenzi, Alexandra McLaughlin, Tom Caron, Morgan Conyer, Pooja Desai, Andrew Schofield, Brittany Barron, Scarlett Peterson, and Faith Thompson. Thank you for being a brave, bold group of bad-ass writers and poets. Your feedback on several of the works included in this collection was both crucial and appreciated.

Notes

SKINNED

Demographers and researchers predict: Stef W. Kite, "Future Fore-told: A New America in 2040," *Axios*, May 21, 2019, https://www.axios .com/being-30-in-2040-future-new-world-us-diversity-2d3ba6db -3345-4ec4-97a8-9282fe1cee67.html; William H. Frey, "The US Will Become 'Minority White' in 2045, Census Projects," *The Avenue* (blog), Brookings Institute, March 14, 2018, https://www.brookings.edu/blog /the-avenue/2018/03/14/the-us-will-become-minority-white-in-2045 -census-projects/.

QUINTONIO'S LOT

Michael's lifeless body: Michael Brown, age eighteen, was shot and killed in Ferguson, Missouri, by a white policeman on August 9, 2014. After the shooting, Brown's body was left in the street for four hours. "Timeline of Events in Shooting of Michael Brown in Ferguson," *Associated Press*, August 8, 2019, https://apnews.com /9aa32033692547699a3b61da8fd1fc62.

Tamir struck down: Tamir Rice, age twelve, was shot and killed at a public playground in Cleveland, Ohio, by a white policeman on November 22, 2014. Officer Loehmann shot Rice within two sec-onds of exiting his police cruiser. Eric Heisig, "Tamir Rice Shooting: A Breakdown of the Events That Led to the 12-year-old's Death," Cleveland.com, January 13, 2017, updated January 11, 2019, https://

www.cleveland.com/court-justice/2017/01/tamir_rice_shooting_a
_breakdow.html.

A brute in policeman's clothing hurl a black daughter: Tim Stelloh and Tracy Connor, "Video Shows Cop Body-Slamming High School Girl in S.C. Classroom," *NBC News*, October 26, 2015, updated October 27, 2015, https://www.nbcnews.com/news/us-news/video-appears-show -cop-body-slamming-student-s-c-classroom-n451896.

Writer Liza Long penned a powerful essay: Liza Long, "'I Am Adam Lanza's Mother': A Mom's Perspective on the Mental Illness Conversation in America," *HuffPost*, December 16, 2012, updated May 13, 2014, https://www.huffpost.com/entry/i-am-adam-lanzas-mother-mental -illness-conversation_n_2311009.

According to *Chicago Tribune* reports: Patrick M. O'Connell and Tony Briscoe, "Families of Two Fatally Shot Call for Police to Improve Interaction," *Chicago Tribune*, December 28, 2015, https://www.chicagotribune .com/news/ct-chicago-police-shooting-update-met-20151227-story .html; Dan Hinkel, "Chicago Police Watchdog Rules 2015 Shooting of Quintonio LeGrier and Bettie Jones Was Unjustified," *Chicago Tribune*, December 29, 2017, https://www.chicagotribune.com/news/breaking /ct-met-legrier-jones-shooting-unjustified-20171228-story.html.

CONGRATULATIONS

Alton Sterling and Philando Castile were gunned down: Alton Sterling, thirty-seven years old, was shot and killed by a white policeman in Baton Rouge, Louisiana, on July 5, 2016. Philando Castile, thirty-two years old, was shot and killed in his car by a Latino policeman in Falcon Heights, Minnesota, on July 6, 2016. His girlfriend and her four-year-old daughter were in the car with him when he was killed. Catherine E. Shoichet, Joshua Berlinger, and Steve Almasy, "Alton Sterling Shooting: Second Video of Deadly Encounter Emerges," *CNN*, updated July 6, 2016, https://www.cnn.com/2016/07/06/us/baton -rouge-shooting-alton-sterling/index.html; Jay Croft, "Philando Castile

Shooting: Dashcam Video Shows Rapid Event," *CNN*, updated July 21, 2017, https://www.cnn.com/2017/06/20/us/philando-castile-shooting-dashcam/index.html.

Homesick

Fetty Wap's injured eye: As a child, rapper Fetty Wap lost his left eye to congenital glaucoma.

Dear Mary

To Mary J. Blige.

American Mourning

Columbine, Virginia Tech, and Newtown: On April 20, 1999, students Eric Harris and Dylan Klebold killed thirteen people, including themselves, and wounded twenty-one others in a shooting at Columbine High School in Littleton, Colorado. On April 16, 2017, undergraduate student Seung-Hui Cho killed thirty-three people, including himself, and wounded seventeen others in a shooting at Virginia Polytechnic Institute and State University in Blacksburg, Virginia. On December 14, 2012, twenty-year-old Adam Lanza shot and killed his mother, then drove to Sandy Hook Elementary School in Newtown, Connecticut, where he killed twenty children under the age of seven, six staff members, and himself.

Low Country Lamentation

Walter Scott had been arrested: Jamiles Lartey, "Former Officer Michael Slager Sentenced to Twenty Years for Murder of Walter Scott," December 7, 2017, https://www.theguardian.com/us-news/2017/dec/07/michael-slager-walter-scott-second-degree-murder.

On Football, Freedom, and Fear

"I give the most strength to my children . . .": Audre Lorde, *Sister Outsider* (Berkeley: Crossing Press, 1984), 72.

Shame the Devil

Emmett Till was kidnapped and murdered: "Emmett Till Is Murdered," *History*, February 9, 2010, updated August 29, 2019, https://www.history .com/this-day-in-history/the-death-of-emmett-till.

An entire Florida town was reduced to ashes: Rosalind Bentley, "The Rosewood Massacre: How a Lie Destroyed a Black Town," *The Atlanta Journal Constitution*, February 17, 2017, https://www.ajc.com/news /national/the-rosewood-massacre-how-lie-destroyed-black-town /wTcKjELkGskePsWiwutQuO/; Trevor Goodloe, "Rosewood Massacre (1923)," BlackPast, March 23, 2008, https://www.blackpast.org /african-american-history/rosewood-massacre-1923/.

Harvey Weinstein: "Harvey Weinstein Timeline: How the Scandal Unfolded," *BBC*, updated December 20, 2019, https://www.bbc.com /news/entertainment-arts-41594672.

Tavis Smiley: Daniel Holloway, "PBS Suspends 'Tavis Smiley' Following Sexual Misconduct Investigation," *Variety*, December 13, 2017, https:// variety.com/2017/tv/news/tavis-smiley-pbs-1202639424/.

Al Franken: John Haltiwanger, "Ninth Woman Accuses Former Sen. Al Franken of Sexual Harassment as He Steps Back into the Public Eye," *Business Insider*, September 30, 2019, https://www.businessinsider .com/ninth-woman-accuses-former-sen-al-franken-of-sexual -harassment-2019-9.

Kevin Spacey: "Kevin Spacey Timeline: How the Story Unfolded," *BBC*, July 18, 2019, https://www.bbc.com/news/entertainment-arts -41884878.

Russell Simmons: Elias Leight, "Russell Simmons Sexual Assault Allegations: A Timeline," *Rolling Stone*, February 9, 2018, https://www.rollingstone.com/music/music-news/russell-simmons-sexual-assault-allegations-a-timeline-202515/.

Charlie Rose: James Oliver Cury, "Charlie Rose's Life Now: 'Broken,' 'Brilliant' and 'Lonely,'" *The Hollywood Reporter*, April 12, 2018, https://www.hollywoodreporter.com/features/what-happened-charlie-rose-we-asked-his-friends-associates-1101333.

Roy Moore: Stephanie McCrummen, Beth Reinhard, and Alice Crites, "Woman Says Roy Moore Initiated Sexual Encounter when She Was Fourteen, He Was Thirty-Two," *The Washington Post*, November 9, 2017, https://www.washingtonpost.com/investigations/woman-says-roy-moore-initiated-sexual-encounter-when-she-was-14-he-was-32/2017/11/09/1f495878-c293-11e7-afe9-4f60b5a6c4a0_story.html.

Matt Lauer: Caitlin Flanagan, "Matt Lauer's Woman Problem," *The Atlantic*, November 5, 2019, https://www.theatlantic.com/ideas/archive/2019/11/lauer-had-a-problem-with-women/601405/.

ALWAYS IN APRIL

Snake charming as a practice was officially banned: Binay Singh, "More Trouble in Store for Snake Charmers," *The Times of India*, updated July 12, 2011, https://timesofindia.indiatimes.com/city/varanasi/More-trouble-in-store-for-snake-charmers/articleshow/9201340.cms.

John Wilkes Booth: On April 14, 1865, John Wilkes Booth assassinated President Abraham Lincoln at Ford's Theatre in Washington, DC.

James Earl Ray: On April 4, 1968, James Earl Ray assassinated Martin Luther King Jr. at the Lorraine Motel in Memphis, Tennessee.

In 2015, at least five people died: "List of Fatal Snake Bites in the United States," Wikipedia, accessed December 10, 2019, https://en.wikipedia.org/wiki/List_of_fatal_snake_bites_in_the_United_States.

CARMEL CLAY PUBLIC LIBRARY

8   02216 6947

CARMEL CLAY PUBLIC LIBRARY
Renewal Line: (317) 814-3936
www.carmel.lib.in.us

CPSIA information can be obtained
at www.ICGtesting.com
Printed in the USA
LVHW092015280920
667305LV00008B/1642

9 781949 259094